Critical Guides to French Texts

Critical Guides to French Texts

EDITED BY ROGER LITTLE, WOLFGANG VAN EMDEN, DAVID WILLIAMS

CREBILLON FILS

Les Egarements du cœur et de l'esprit

Patrick Fein

Professor of French
Rhodes University, Grahamstown

Grant & Cutler Ltd
2000

ISBN 0 7293 0416 7

DEPÓSITO LEGAL: V. 4.644 - 2000

Printed in Spain by
Artes Gráficas Soler, S.A., Valencia
for
GRANT & CUTLER LTD
55-57 GREAT MARLBOROUGH STREET, LONDON W1V 2AY

Contents

Contents

References

References to the text of *Les Egarements du cœur et de l'esprit* are to the edition by Jean Dagen (Paris, Garnier-Flammarion, 1985). This edition contains an Introduction, notes and a chronological outline of Crébillon's life.

References to works listed in the Select Bibliography give the italicised number ascribed there to that work, followed by the relevant page-number.

Acknowledgements

I am indebted to the Joint Research Committee of Rhodes University for a research grant and to the French Embassy at Pretoria for a senior research scholarship which enabled me to visit France and England to consult with colleagues specialised in the field, and also relevant material in Library collections in those countries.

I have benefited from the help and advice of many colleagues and friends, notably Colette Cazenobe, William Barber, Jean Dagen, Michel Delon, Michel Gilot, Robert Niklaus and Jean Sgard, to whom I should like to register my gratitude.

1. Introduction

Les Egarements du cœur et de l'esprit (1736-38) has generally been considered as Crébillon's most successful novel, and contains in its preface his main statement of his aims as a practitioner of the genre. The contrast between *coeur* and *esprit*, that is the feelings of the heart as opposed to reason, is a familiar one in the eighteenth century and the balance to be achieved is never decisive between sensibility and *libertinage*; the notion of *égarement* is that of an aberration or error that needs to be perceived by the individual before a balanced attitude and behaviour can be regained.

The theme of an adolescent initiated into society provides Crébillon with an opportunity to depict and satirise that society, a satire here associated with the theme frequently developed in French literature of the sentimental education of an adolescent by an older woman, as depicted by Flaubert in his *Education sentimentale* (1869) or Colette in *Le Blé en herbe* (1923), in which she explores the budding relationship of two young people in a middle-class French milieu, set against the sexual manipulation of an older woman.

The form of *Les Egarements* attains a classical perfection despite its unfinished state. The novel was published in three parts, the first in Paris in 1736, the two others at The Hague in 1738. A conclusion, mentioned in the preface, which was to show the hero saved from the libertine life by an estimable woman, was never published. Through discourse and behaviour, a libertine code is defined that will serve as a code of practice even as late as 1782 in Laclos's *Les Liaisons dangereuses*.

The dialogue reflects the tone of the 'extrêmement bonne compagnie' in the *salons* Crébillon frequented from an early age. The use of dialogue as a weapon of seduction portrayed so effectively in *Les Egarements* is a recurring feature in Crébillon's work, and he did in fact publish two dialogues almost as a geometric demonstration of the method employed by the libertine, whether male or female.

La Nuit et le moment ou les Matines de Cythère, a dialogue
between Clitandre and Cidalise during one night in her bedroom,
appeared in 1755, but was first written between 1737 and 1745 and
probably later revised. *Le Hasard du coin du feu, dialogue moral*
was published in 1763 and originally conceived around 1742. This
second dialogue takes place between the Duc and Célie, who takes
the initiative and attempts to detach him from his current mistress,
but resignedly accepts that her seduction has succeeded only to the
extent that he will have to be shared with her rival, a conclusion
perhaps more in keeping with the permissiveness of the period when
it was written than with the 1760s.

It has already been noted that the balance to be achieved
between sensibility, that is *sentiment*, and *libertinage* is never
decisive and varies throughout the period of the eighteenth century.
There is evidence of sensibility in the novel before 1720, its origins
being closely linked to the tradition of the *salons*. Sensibility, for the
major novelists, Prévost, Marivaux, Diderot and Rousseau, was
reflected in the importance given to feeling, the study of feelings,
reflection on the emotions and accentuating them to allow refined
and detailed analysis. The novel of sensibility was popularised by
Richardson in both England and France, followed by Jean-Jacques
Rousseau, the foremost pre-Romantic novelist of the period, with the
publication of *La Nouvelle Héloïse* (1761).

It is known that Claude Crébillon was born in Paris on 14
February 1707. His father had already achieved some success in
writing plays for the classical tragic theatre in the tradition of Racine,
a genre in which he competed with Voltaire. Little is known of
Claude Crébillon's mother, except that she gave birth two weeks
after her marriage and that she died four years later. The son was
educated by the Jesuits and his teachers thought sufficiently highly
of him to suggest that he should enter their Order. His refusal was no
doubt partly based on temperament; while the father was taciturn and
misanthropic, the son was light-hearted and witty.

Crébillon was clearly anxious to become acquainted with
polite society and, thanks to his father's reputation as a dramatist, he
was admitted to the *salons* of Sceaux and Saint-Germain at an early
age in the last years of the Regency (1715-23), during the minority
of Louis XV, great-grandson of Louis XIV. He was much affected

by this period of unrestrained pleasure, like Voltaire who also regarded it as the best period of his life. In the case of Crébillon, the fictional works he later wrote used Versailles and Paris at the time of the Regency as a setting and reflected its tone.

The Duc de Saint-Simon, from the viewpoint of his exalted position at the court of Louis XIV, depicted in his *Mémoires* (1694-1723) aristocratic society at the end of that long reign and under the subsequent Regency. The aristocratic class had left the provinces for the attractions of court life at Versailles, where they lived in bored idleness enlivened by balls, gambling and entertainments commissioned by artists of the period. The *ennui* felt by a military caste whose social purpose had ended is one explanation for the mentality they developed and which perished with the Revolution of 1789. It is an aspect that Crébillon was to illustrate through the characters of *Les Egarements*, as well as his other works.

The *libertins* or free-thinkers of the seventeenth century developed into the *roués* of the Regency. This term, initially used for those sentenced to the capital punishment of being broken on a wheel for various crimes including atheism and sexual perversion, was taken up by the debauched inner circle of the Regent's court, whose leader was the Maréchal Duc de Richelieu, and they applied it to themselves as libertines.

The young Crébillon also had his entrée backstage to the Comédie Française, the Comédie Italienne and the Théâtre de la Foire. However, it was the *salons* and not the theatre that most influenced the future novelist and at the age of twenty-three he wrote *Le Sylphe ou Songe de Madame de R...*, a *conte* that introduces the *petit-maître*, in the form of an imaginary sylph. The term *petit-maître*, with its origins in the sixteenth century, remained fashionable throughout the eighteenth century to designate, in Voltaire's phrase, 'la jeunesse impertinente et mal élevée' within court society. Crébillon satirises the type, both in its masculine and feminine representations, throughout his work and such characters play an important role in *Les Egarements*.

What is perhaps surprising is how little is known to us about Crébillon's relationships with women, since the analysis of feminine psychology is at the centre of his work, his feminine characters representing the range of types to be observed within society. Contemporaries mention Mademoiselle Gaussin, an actress to whom Crébillon is said to have proposed marriage and who first accepted then rejected him in favour of an arrangement with a rich *fermier-général*. When Crébillon married, he chose Henriette-Marie Stafford, grand-daughter of a Chamberlain at the Court of James II and born and brought up in exile at Saint-Germain-en-Laye.

In 1750, Crébillon left Paris for Sens, south-east of the capital, for reasons of economy, and then moved to Saint-Germain to occupy borrowed accommodation, where Madame Crébillon died in 1756, after bearing a son who died in childhood. Thanks to the support of Madame de Pompadour, mistress of Louis XV, in 1759 Crébillon was named Royal Censor, a post held earlier by his father, and apparently he carried out his function of judging works for publication with conscientiousness.

The last novel definitively attributed to Crébillon appeared in 1771, when he was sixty-four years of age. The *Lettres athéniennes extraites du portefeuille d'Alcibiade*, as the title implies, is an epistolary novel with a classical Greek setting, a transposition of eighteenth-century French aristocratic society. The work is lengthy and rambling because Crébillon, in using a form for his novel that had remained popular since the *Lettres portugaises* (1669) by Guilleragues, did not display the technique that Laclos demonstrated only eleven years later in 1782 in writing his *Liaisons dangereuses* of reducing the correspondence to the essential intrigue. Nevertheless, Alcibiade is a complex figure in the tradition of Crébillon's libertines, with a cynical vanity and lust for domination that make him a precursor of Valmont, while his relationship with the courtesan Némée anticipates the strategy of Valmont and Merteuil, the accomplices in Laclos's novel.

Crébillon then fell silent and devoted himself to his work as Censor, dying in poverty and buried without ceremony at Saint-Germain l'Auxerrois. He died indebted to his tailor, his bookseller and various lawyers, but his cellar still contained some five hundred bottles of wine, the mark of the bon viveur who had been a leading member of the dining-club named the *Caveau*.

Crébillon's social life had included contact with literary figures at various levels. They influenced his literary work and refer to him in their correspondence. He was one of the founding members of the *Caveau*, which took its name from the hostelry in the rue de Buci where Crébillon, Collé, a friend from childhood days, and Piron dined regularly twice a month and subsequently every Sunday. These gatherings expanded to become literary dinners where members freely discussed their current works, gossiped, made up epigrams and satirical verse and generally exercised their wit at the expense of their colleagues and the authorities. The reader of *Les Egarements* obtains some idea of the repartee of *salon* conversation, as also of the wit that Crébillon was known to display in social gatherings. The club lasted for a ten-year period and then gradually ceased to function as its reputation spread and society people attended merely to observe the scurrilous witticisms enjoyed by this artistic gathering.

Crébillon moved in various social circles and between 1742 and 1745 he was particularly well known to the novelist Mme de Graffigny. After his detention for five days at the Château de Vincennes in 1734 at the request of the Duchesse du Maine, as a result of the political satire contained in his novel *L'Ecumoire, ou Tanzaï et Néadarné, histoire japonaise* (1734), Crébillon had been ordered to publish nothing without official authorisation. The publication of *Le Sopha* in 1742 led to his exile from Paris, since contemporaries saw in certain characters, an impotent libertine and his accomplice, references to the Maréchal Duc de Richelieu and the Duc de Nivernais. These were powerful personalities, the latter being brother-in-law to the minister Maurepas, who was empowered to sign detention and restriction orders. After written supplication, the order was revoked three months later and Crébillon was permitted to return to Paris. However, he became discouraged from writing and did not publish further for ten years.

As Crébillon was in the habit of reading his works to literary friends before he regarded them as fit for publication, much of his later work was conceived at an earlier date and published only after revisions. This practice of reading his works aloud was probably a factor in the personal style that he evolved. It is also known that Crébillon was quite capable of imitating the style of other writers. As an example of this, the *Vie de Marianne* of Marivaux had begun to appear in 1731, three years before *L'Ecumoire*. Crébillon devoted three chapters of his novel to a critique of Marivaux's style, writing a pastiche, interrupting the flow of the *récit* with reflections and including remarks on the art of story-telling apparently for the benefit of Marivaux.

Crébillon habitually read his work to Duclos, a minor author writing mainly within the libertine genre, and there is evidence from Mme de Graffigny that Crébillon had subsequently written three further parts to provide a conclusion for *Les Egarements du cœur et de l'esprit*, that he intended to read these to Duclos, but he had not yet done so by June 1743. While the Preface published with the first part of the text in 1736 proposes a moral conclusion to Meilcour's memoirs, with the reform of the hero thanks to an estimable woman, this conclusion never appeared and the novel remained unfinished. It is quite possible that Crébillon felt that such a conclusion had already been published by Duclos in his *Confessions du Comte de* *** (1741). The first part is an example of the *roman-liste*, enumerating the hero's conquests in various classes of society, in France and abroad, but in the second part the estimable Madame de Selve saves the Comte from 'l'ivresse impétueuse des sens' and replaces desire by friendship, tenderness and esteem.

The popularity of Crébillon's work varied at different periods of the eighteenth century. What is indisputable is that he was one of the most widely read of authors with twenty-nine editions of *Les Egarements du cœur et de l'esprit* published between 1738 and the Revolution of 1789 (*33*, p.16). The Abbé Desfontaines regarded the text as frivolous, but ingenious and amusing. Palissot considered Crébillon as an 'écrivain d'un mérite très rare'. However, critical opinion turned against Crébillon's works, particularly against the later works published between 1754 and 1771, and he came to be regarded, like Marivaux, as a writer who had outlived his reputation, precisely echoing the opinion of Diderot in *Le Neveu de Rameau*.

Although we now know that Crébillon never visited England, he was widely read there. He was well acquainted with prominent English persons whom he welcomed in France. Not only was the last edition of Crébillon's complete works published in London in 1777, testifying to a wide readership there, but he was also appreciated by writers such as Walpole, Gray, Hume, Wilkes and Sterne, who declared that it was only after reading Rabelais and Crébillon that he decided to take up the pen.

Crébillon's reputation in the nineteenth century remained at the low level determined by the French literary critics at the end of the previous century, based primarily on moralistic judgments, and no critical edition of his works appeared. There are a few exceptions of note, such as Stendhal in his *De l'amour*, who rightly saw Crébillon as the originator of the concept of *amour-goût*. Sainte-Beuve also gives Crébillon his approbation in a few brief phrases. However, it was not until the Lièvre edition of the *Œuvres complètes* (even though incomplete) of 1929-30 that Crébillon's rehabilitation began to establish itself, continuing in the second half of the twentieth century as moral certainties of a previous generation were gradually eroded. (A further edition of the text, with a preface by Seylaz, was published by Eds Rencontre of Lausanne in 1956.) The literary and pedagogic value of the novel was officially established forty years ago when it appeared on the syllabus of the Licence at certain French universities and in the B.A. programme at some British universities, and its reputation was confirmed when it appeared on the syllabus of the *Agrégation* for the 1995-96 academic year, the French Ministry of Education responding to the new revival of interest in an author mistakenly dismissed as erotic by an earlier generation of critics with narrow conceptions of morality. Crébillon was himself an upright man, not known as a libertine, and his work depicted a section of society, without necessarily approving of its behaviour.

While views on morality changed, there are also literary explanations for a revived interest in Crébillon and *Les Egarements*, in particular the new interest in narratology and interpretations of the eighteenth-century novels written in the memoir form. William Edmiston[1] comments interestingly on the 'selective focalization' of the narrator Meilcour telling his story in *Les Egarements*:

---

[1] William F. Edmiston, 'Selective focalization and *égarement* in Crébillon's *Les Egarements du cœur et de l'esprit*', *French Review*, 63, 1989, 45-56.

An older man sits down to record the experiences of a
two-week period in his youth and his relations with
several members of his society. Despite the constraints
imposed upon him by convention, the narrator often
takes liberties with his focal limitations and gives
information that he cannot naturally possess. More
important, he also chooses to ignore his temporal
advantage and to withhold information that he should
possess. In viewing certain characters in the novel, the
reader follows the consciousness of the narrator and is
thus privy to all of the knowledge of the older man. At
the same time the reader's understanding of other
characters is limited, and strictly so, to only the
knowledge of the young Meilcour. The effect of this
selective focalization, focal variation between the
narrating self and the experiencing self, is to create a
certain confusion in the mind of the reader, which is
essential to an understanding of the puzzlement of the
poor hero trying to cope with an ambiguous and often
false society.

The movement between Meilcour the narrator and the youth
Meilcour involved in the events has all the advantages and
limitations of the memoir form. This has been analysed by Gérard
Genette and others using the theory of narratology and its specific
vocabulary, such as the term focalization itself. His inexperienced
relations with other characters tend even to confuse the reader's
interpretation of events and motives. Other critics, such as Vivienne
Mylne, Philip Stewart and Peter Brooks, have commented on the
way that Crébillon uses his narrator to describe the past, to analyse
himself as he was.

Vivienne Mylne comments on narrative procedure in *Les
Egarements* that she regards as innovative, in particular an
omniscience on the part of the narrator forced upon Crébillon by his
preoccupation with the analysis of feelings. Consequently, 'the
duplicity, scheming and secret intentions of the characters
surrounding Meilcour are vital to the plot and, in Crébillon's eyes,
interesting in themselves. They must therefore be conveyed to the

reader. Meilcour is the only mouthpiece of the novel, so that even if he is supposedly too young and simple to know what his associates are thinking, it is still through him that this information must reach us. In the circumstances, it is hardly surprising that Crébillon has slipped over the brink into omniscience' (*29*, pp.133-34).

Philip Stewart sees the narrator Meilcour as an apprentice in 'la parfaite habileté civile des gens du monde', which needs to be learned, and *Les Egarements* as the story of that education, so that passages of omniscient penetration are no more than ironic hindsight, with no pretence of objectivity or accuracy (*35*, p.160).

Peter Brooks observes that 'the narrative structure of the novel closely controls our reactions as readers. Not only does the narrative tone preclude any sentimentality or naive moralism on our part, the structural distance between Meilcour-as-narrator and Meilcour-as-protagonist defines the distance at which we must hold characters and action, determines that we shall view them with the distanced, defining and evaluative language of the portrait' (*15*, p.32). Meilcour the narrator has gained worldly knowledge that permits him to reconstruct the past psychology of the characters portrayed and that is the purpose of his education.

It must be added that the theme of *Les Egarements* centres on Meilcour's romantic interest shared between the older woman Madame de Lursay and the young girl Hortense de Théville. The reader sees them entirely through the eyes of the narrator and there is a variance of treatment between Madame de Lursay, whose motives are clarified, and Hortense, who remains as obscure as when the young uninitiated Meilcour fell in love with her. The narrator's comments are primarily used to accentuate the ridiculous aspects of the protagonist's misconceptions and behaviour and to satirise the society that he is to enter.

The behaviour of that society was in any case influenced by currents of thought prevalent in the period in which Crébillon lived. In her analysis of 'La *Leçon de l'étoile* dans *Les Egarements*', Carole Dornier begins by pointing out that the information given to Meilcour by Versac is essentially founded on general principles formulated as precepts (*20*, pp.266-67). She goes on to remark that 'le mentor des *Egarements* inculque à son élève une conception de l'honnêteté où le respect des bienséances l'emporte sur celui des règles morales. Son pragmatisme se ressent à la fois d'une tradition aristocratique, celle du *Cortegiano* (de Baldassarre Castiglione, 1528) qui doit se déguiser sans cesse, et d'un utilitarisme qui se développera au cours du XVIIIe siècle...' (*20*, pp.268-69). Jean Lafond's work *La Rochefoucauld, augustinisme et littérature* (Paris, Klincksieck, 1977, p. 194) is referred to as showing *pessimisme augustinien* as 'le point de départ et l'assise d'un système où le négatif est subitement transmué en positif... l'amour-propre en instrument efficace du bonheur sur terre' (*20*, p.269). The *Cortegiano*, or *Courtier*, serves as a manual of aristocratic behaviour throughout Europe from its publication in the early sixteenth century.

It becomes clear from the development of Versac's lesson that he is influenced by the Duc de La Rochefoucauld (1613-80), author of the *Maximes* (1665), and pessimism based on theological concepts of Jansenist pre-determinism. He shares with the French seventeenth-century classical moralists a disillusioned view of the world and a conception of *honnêteté* that is not in keeping with worldly success based on self-interest. The frequent stylistic recourse to the maxim, judgment, aphorism, reflection on human behaviour within society shows Crébillon's debt to these moralists, La Rochefoucauld and La Bruyère (1645-96), author of the *Caractères* (1688).

In association with pessimism and self-interest may be seen a deterministic view of man's situation and nature, a belief shared by all of Crébillon's libertines. Alcibiade, in the *Lettres athéniennes*, is convinced that human reactions are not individualised, that they are subject to inexorable laws, since people do not change. Alcibiade writes to Antipe: 'La fureur des conquêtes est en moi, comme est en vous la jalousie, un vice de caractère; et vous n'ignorez pas que, si quelquefois ces vices se suspendent, on n'en triomphe jamais. Toute la différence que j'imagine entre vous et moi, c'est que la nature vous a fait ce que vous êtes, et que si je ne me raidissais pas contre ses impulsions, c'est-à-dire qu'en moi l'esprit ne corrompît point le cœur, je ne serais pas ce que je suis' (*12*).

Versac, in *Les Egarements*, claims to have made himself what he is, an accomplished *petit-maître*, which distinguishes him from lesser men around him, and he proposes to explain to Meilcour the principles that will allow the young man to follow the same path. Crébillon indicates in the Preface to the text that Meilcour will become 'un homme plein de fausses idées, et pétri de ridicules, et qui y est moins entraîné encore par lui-même, que par des personnes intéressées à lui corrompre le cœur et l'esprit' (pp.67-68). It is improbable that there can be any turning back in such a career and it is even probable that Crébillon had little faith in the powers of the 'estimable woman', however she might be portrayed, to return Meilcour to the path of virtue. The laws determined by society have already prevented Meilcour from following his heart towards the inaccessible Hortense; he is seduced by Madame de Lursay, but society will require that he is 'formed' for entry into society by Madame de Senanges, much against his own inclination.

Meilcour concludes in the final scene of the novel that sentiment as he has experienced it is a questionable basis for his future conduct: what he names 'le quiétisme de l'amour' (p. 248), allowing him to reconcile his love for Hortense with his sexual relationship with Madame de Lursay, and which he now accepts as inevitable, indicates the illusory nature of personal freedom to follow his own sincere inclinations rather than conform with the behaviour of his society.

This conclusion leads Crébillon to dissect lucidly the motivations and the behaviour of a section of the society of his time and to bring out the ultimate emptiness of the exercise of seduction, thus implying a certain contempt for those who devote their lives to it. We know that Richardson, writing for a different audience in England and expressing a bourgeois morality, refused to make an atheist of Lovelace, the hero of his novel *Clarissa Harlowe* (1747), even though he does express opinions in favour of reason and scepticism. Crébillon's libertines are sceptical of apparent human motivation, in the tradition of the French classical moralists, and, seeing themselves as part of a vicious society in the process of inevitable decline, seek to define conceptions of virtue taken from an earlier historical period. However, at no time do they express religious ideas: the latter are entirely absent from their thinking, in contrast with Laclos's Valmont, who wishes to take the place of the

Christian God in the mind of Madame de Tourvel as proof of his final domination over her.

Robert Niklaus, in his article on Crébillon and Richardson, (*30*, p.1172) asks the pertinent question: 'Qu'est-ce donc que le libertin du XVIIIe siècle?', and he responds with the definition that the typical figure must be seen as a rationalist free-thinker, seeking sensation in his search for happiness, 'un jouisseur qui craint la passion et tout ce qui échappe au contrôle de l'esprit, un homme inconstant par devoir, qui joue des rôles sensiblement différents au cours du siècle'. In this portrait, we see Crébillon as being influenced in his characterisation by the hedonistic aspect of the Regency period: he sees love as reduced to phenomena of attraction, he analyses love as *amour-goût* and perhaps regrets that such a deterministic view of psychology is unlikely fully to satisfy the heart, the mind and the senses. With the character of Versac, Crébillon shows the prototype of the libertine who exposes the weakness of the flesh through his multiple seductions, who lives through sensation and yet believes in total control of himself and others, who comes to wear a mask in society and finds himself essentially dissatisfied with his existence. Such a libertine cast of mind will later be depicted and developed by Crébillon in such characters as Alcibiade and then by Laclos and Sade.

It must be said that Crébillon's most successful endeavour to depict the behaviour of a particular section of the society of his time was in *Les Egarements du cœur et de l'esprit*. Etiemble, who has done so much to restore this text to its rightful place among eighteenth-century French novels, comments on the economy of structure that is used to describe the initiation of a young nobleman under the tutelage of the libertine Versac. The sentimental education provided by his feelings for the mature but still very attractive Madame de Lursay, the young girl Hortense de Théville, whom he romanticises, and the experienced Madame de Senanges, teaches Meilcour more clearly to understand women, the libertine milieu he is to enter and most importantly himself. Etiemble notes, in his *Romanciers du XVIIIe siècle* (*13*, II, p. xv), the 'structure dramatique' (*Les Egarements* has indeed recently been transferred to the stage)[2] and the 'plan rigoureux' involving 'cinq personnages essentiels...' As he accurately observes, 'supprimez-en un seul, et tout s'écroule...' and 'une intrigue aussi serrée à la fois et concentrée (quinze jours) donne l'heureuse illusion d'un délai interminable'.

As I have indicated elsewhere (*25*, pp.96-97), 'from the standpoint of the role of women, *Les Egarements du cœur et de l'esprit* is the most significant of Crébillon's works. Whilst his main interest is to bring out the character of Meilcour and study his reactions in depth, he can do so only by examining Meilcour's relations with women; and here Crébillon as author has selected his three women with very great care. Though these women are in a sense subordinate, ... in fact they underline the structure of the work ... basically the structure is Meilcour's relations with Madame de Lursay, Hortense de Théville and Madame de Senanges.' Certainly, it is true to say that Meilcour's thoughts and feelings as memorialist are divided between these women, and his reactions to them elucidate the mental processes through which he has to pass to embark on his career as a professional libertine. The novel is a psychological study of *égarement* expressed in a structure of French neo-classical simplicity that has its literary origins in the seventeenth century.

---

[2] Adapted by Eric Lorvoire and staged at the Lucernaire Theatre, Centre National d'Art et d'Essai, in Paris in 1991. The dialogue *La Nuit et le moment* was adapted for the theatre by J.-L. Thamin and performed by the Comédie Française at the Théâtre de l'Odéon during their 1977-78 season. This dialogue was also adapted as a film by A.-M. Tato and appeared in Paris in 1995.

2. Structure and Form

The text of *Les Egarements* is presented as being the memoirs of M. de Meilcour, the middle-aged narrator reformed from his earlier dissolute life-style who gives the reader an account of his entry into society. As a young man of high birth and large fortune, Meilcour seeks to fill the void in his life through the society of women and it is through him that Crébillon introduces the theme of initiation. A female friend of Meilcour's mother, Madame de Lursay, has taken a keen interest in him for six months, seeking to take charge of his sexual education. Since correct behaviour forbids that she should make the first move, she must bring her pupil to declare himself, divided as he is between desire and respect: a difficult situation, which leads to a series of scenes of misunderstanding and an aim that succeeds only in the final scene.

While the plot pursues this course, an alternative presents itself: Meilcour falls passionately in love with the young Hortense de Théville, whom he has every reason to believe is inaccessible to him. These two narrative threads are intertwined. The theme of the heart divided in its object of desire, which essentially provides the intrigue of the novel, does not actually create a situation of conflict. Meilcour's two loves both influence him in such a manner that each woman profits from his feelings for her rival without knowing it, since the indecisive lover attempts to accommodate his divided desires. Madame de Lursay, although so perspicacious and clairvoyant that she always seems to guess what agitates Meilcour's heart, never suspects for a moment the one profound emotion that affects him: his love for Hortense.

As to Meilcour's feelings for the older Madame de Lursay, disillusion comes all too soon: strongly influenced by the admired *petit-maître* Versac, Meilcour surmises that beneath the exterior respectability there hides a woman of much looser morals with a shady past. His immediate reaction is one of contempt for her, in consequence of his disillusion, as the mature woman and mother-figure of his imagination is suddenly revealed as a real woman with her own desires, schemes and vanity.

The moment of disillusion brought about by Versac, in the role of the libertine philosopher, introduces the initiate Meilcour to the philosophic stage of his education. It is the moment of initiation through which a collective secret of his particular caste in society is imparted. The essence of libertinism thus revealed is that all authority is rejected, all social respectability is a camouflage and desire is a means to control.

Removed from her pedestal, Madame de Lursay precedes, in the gallery of corrupt women revealed to Meilcour, the more extravagant Madame de Senanges and Madame de Mongennes, who complete the new image with which Meilcour develops his sentimental education. The young man has entered into society and he is depicted in this novel of worldliness as placing blame on those women who initiate him, at the same time as he views them as the main source of pleasure. He sees in them only seducers who satisfy their own desires. However, his contempt gives him at last the necessary boldness to initiate a situation in which Madame de Lursay can give him his first practical lesson in love, even though he still desires to involve himself with Hortense. Everything in these memoirs leads to the sexual scene of the conclusion. But Madame de Lursay will not suffice for the initiation, Madame de Senanges in her turn will bring to Meilcour her experience, although in a future beyond the scope of these memoirs. The chronology of the text and a plan of its structure can be found in the helpful critical work by Dagen (*19*, pp.84-100).

Crébillon chose the form of the memoir-novel in writing *Les Egarements du cœur et de l'esprit*. It was after the memoir-novel had become established as the predominant form of French fiction that the letter-form came into vogue in the mid-eighteenth century and Rousseau was to choose it for his enormously popular *La Nouvelle Héloïse* (1761). However, the genre of the letter-novel had already proved popular when Guilleragues published the *Lettres portugaises* (1669) and Montesquieu developed the form with his *Lettres persanes* (1721), an imaginary correspondence between two Persian notables, one of whom is visiting France. Crébillon had already published the *Lettres de la Marquise de M... au Comte de R...* in 1732 before he began publishing *Les Egarements* in 1736, so his choice of the memoir-novel form for the latter work is therefore significant. Also noteworthy is the admission, contrary to contemporary fashion, that memoirs may be invented: 'soit qu'on doive les regarder comme un ouvrage purement d'imagination, ou que les aventures qu'ils contiennent soient réelles' (Préface, p.65).

The *roman-mémoire* does in fact constitute a unique exception in Crébillon's work, apart from any comparison that might be made with *Les Heureux Orphelins* (1754), which consists of a third-person narrative, a story in memoir-form and a sequence of letters. The question may therefore be asked as to why Crébillon chose the form of the memoir to recount Meilcour's experiences. The short answer is that, in a novel of initiation, this form of expression enables Crébillon to describe society through the eyes of a young man being introduced to its complexities, as well as permitting comment by the older Meilcour as explanation of what is unclear to the initiate, the primary purpose of the psychological novel being the perception of nuances of thought and feeling.

In a novel of sentimental education, the form of the memoir allows the interpretation of behaviour of a *salon* society controlled by women, who formulate the rules to be observed in the social game of seduction. Crébillon had been preceded in this theme by Prévost with *Manon Lescaut* and by Marivaux with *La Vie de Marianne* (both 1731) but their authors' aims were different. It may even be said that Crébillon's aim was more limited, namely the education of a young man who would become the disciple of the *petit-maître* Versac, and his introduction to the values of *libertinage*. Prévost introduces the Chevalier des Grieux to Manon and the passion of love, which obliges him to earn money to keep his flighty mistress and gain experience of various levels of society. Marivaux describes the problems of Marianne attempting to find an entrée into society while suffering the misfortune of being orphaned without proof of noble origins. By contrast, Meilcour's place is assured. In a restricted society, he has all the qualities required of birth and wealth, and needs only to learn the rules to become a libertine in the style of Versac. An obvious comparison may be made with Duclos's *Les Confessions du comte de ...* (1741), which takes the form of a *roman-liste* of the Comte's conquests followed by his redemption by the estimable Madame de Selve.

Crébillon's novel remains unfinished. In a sense, the form of the memoir-novel implies the impossibility of concluding with the death of the memorialist. It may even be reasonable to assume that Crébillon regarded his novel as being satisfactorily concluded and that rumours of his having written further sections of the novel were without foundation. The main evidence for believing in the existence of further unpublished parts comes from the correspondence of Mme de Graffigny, where she refers to three further parts that he had written, but was unwilling, or too lazy in her view, to prepare for publication (*4*, pp.75 and 193).

Marivaux, for his part, abandoned Marianne as a young girl apparently far from achieving her intention of becoming the Comtesse de ..., who supposedly writes the memoirs. Crébillon may well have thought the young Meilcour, sexually initiated by Madame de Lursay, too distant from his further education by Madame de Senanges and certainly a long way from being reformed by an estimable woman. Such a conclusion, in any case, would merely duplicate the ending of Duclos's novel *Les Confessions du comte de...*, already published in 1741 before Mme de Graffigny alludes to a continuation of *Les Egarements* in 1743 and 1744. It could also be suggested that Crébillon had come to see the present ending as more psychologically realistic. As the novel stands, by the end of the third part it is complete, Meilcour is set on his career as a libertine, it would be superfluous for Crébillon to duplicate his character Versac, and Meilcour understands sufficiently clearly the motivations of those around him, except those of Hortense, who remains in a shadowy dream-world of unreality, in contrast with the sexually available reality of Madame de Lursay.

We may well conclude that Crébillon's decision not to publish more of Meilcour's adventures was based on other considerations, other works to write, such as the pseudo-oriental tale *Le Sopha*, published in 1742. His predilection, in any case, was for short works like the *Dialogues*, which date from this period, and he would not have wished to emulate Marivaux, whose *Vie de Marianne* still remained unfinished at the end of eleven parts. Although apparently unfinished, *Les Egarements du cœur et de l'esprit*, as a novel of initiation, reaches a satisfactory conclusion with Meilcour's loss of virginity and loss of illusions.

What is presumably implied by initiation is loss of innocence and also instruction in a code of conduct. Crébillon's libertines were precursors in defining that same code. *Libertinage* is a game played by members of the aristocracy, a game which expresses in sexual terms the rebellion of the libertine of the sixteenth and seventeenth centuries against the authority of God, religion and the throne. This conception of a game played out by Crébillon's characters is illustrated by the subject-matter of the text, its structure and form and the libertine characters obsessed by winning and demonstrating control over their opponent in clear view of society.

Society feeds the vanity of the libertine, who belongs to a military caste, by according to his successful seductions that *gloire* or admiration attributed by previous generations to military conquests. At the outset of his memoirs, Meilcour understands the importance given to pleasure through women, for he confides to the reader: 'L'idée du plaisir fut, à mon entrée dans le monde, la seule qui m'occupa. La paix, qui régnait alors, me laissait dans un loisir dangereux. Le peu d'occupation, que se font communément les gens de mon rang et de mon âge, le faux air, la liberté, l'exemple, tout m'entraînait vers les plaisirs...' (pp.69-70).

Meilcour therefore seeks 'ce qu'alors les deux sexes nommaient Amour... une sorte de commerce, où l'on s'engageait, souvent même sans goût, où la commodité était toujours préférée à la sympathie, l'intérêt au plaisir, et le vice au sentiment' (p.71). However, his ignorance of the rules, the set movements of the libertine seduction, is a major obstacle. In *libertinage*, there are four main sequences: firstly, there is the choice, Meilcour being drawn initially towards Madame de Lursay, as he sees her frequently and she guardedly makes an effort to attract him, even though he fails to read her repeated signals. It will be Versac who explains to him that, for the purpose of his entry to society, he must choose Madame de Senanges because she will publicise their liaison, while Madame de Lursay, conscious of her reputation, will try to conceal any relationship from the gossip of *le public*, that society of their equals which apportions praise and censure.

Secondly, there is the process of seduction, and it is an innovative aspect of Crébillon's text that makes what is normally a game played according to set rules between two persons mutually agreed and so able rapidly to reach an anticipated conclusion into an apparently interminable series of misunderstandings. A number of aphorisms about the conduct of women at the time when Meilcour was young introduce the story, but these statements come presumably from the older Meilcour with his acquired knowledge: 'J'en ai vu qui, après quinze jours de soins rendus, étaient encore indécises, et dont le mois tout entier n'achevait pas la défaite. Je conviens que ce sont des exemples rares, et qui semblent ne devoir pas tirer à conséquence pour le reste; même, si je ne me trompe, les femmes sévères à ce point-là, passaient pour être un peu prudes' (p.72). However keen Meilcour and Madame de Lursay may be to come together, it takes fourteen days which appear even longer to the reader.

It is the conquest, the third movement, that concludes the third and last part of the novel, and clearly the more experienced Madame de Lursay has finally succeeded in achieving the *dénouement* to mutual satisfaction. While Meilcour has his regrets, because he believes that he has given his heart to Hortense, he is firmly resolved to continue the sexual liaison in which he is involved: 'je la quittai, en lui promettant, malgré mes remords, de la voir le lendemain de bonne heure, très déterminé, de plus, à lui tenir parole' (p.248). As these are the concluding words of the novel as we know it, there is no place for the fourth and final phase of abandonment. We know from the text, since the older Meilcour is in a position to enlighten the reader, that Meilcour will abandon Madame de Lursay in favour of Madame de Senanges. In terms of the libertine code, this action should take place with maximum publicity to ruin the reputation of the victim, the woman concerned, and to give the greatest credit to the reputation of the libertine, in the eyes of *le public*. We can only surmise that Meilcour will have learned the lesson from Versac that the action of abandonment, within the erotic situation, is a metaphor for the control that the seducer exercises over the victim. It could also be seen as a metaphor for Crébillon's control as author, abandoning the reader and falling silent at the point he chooses, leaving unanswered questions as to Meilcour's future.

Meilcour is influenced not only by *libertinage* in his relations with women as he enters society but also by worldliness and the code of behaviour that it requires. Crébillon wrote a novel of manners, described by Peter Brooks as 'a comedy of manners, a novel about social beings and ideas dramatized within a social framework' (*15*, p.13). Worldliness is defined succinctly by Brooks as an ethos which attaches primary importance to life within a public system of values and to the social techniques that further one's position in it.

The comic element that is apparent in the text comes essentially from the ignorance of Meilcour, who is unaware of the social techniques available to him and to Madame de Lursay to bring their relationship to the conclusion they both seek. His extreme timidity prevents him from following her lead, any show of severity on her part discouraging him immediately. Her problem consequently is that, in a *salon* society where everyone is observed, it is more than her reputation is worth to be seen to be making obvious advances to the young man. A code of behaviour in a love-affair, where a glance, a faint blush or fluttering of the eyelids, a sigh, a pressure of the hand, inform the suitor unequivocally that his sentiments are reciprocated, leaves Meilcour baffled and Madame de Lursay is at her wits' end to break through his apparent stupidity. This is most clearly indicated in the celebrated 'scène des nœuds', when she contrives to be alone with him and all he can find to say to her is to comment that he sees she is engaged in a futile pastime of the period (p.122). As it is truly said, 'avec un homme expérimenté, un mot dont le sens même peut se détourner, un regard, un geste, moins encore, le met au fait, s'il veut être aimé; et, supposé qu'il se soit arrangé différemment de ce qu'on souhaiterait, on n'a hasardé que des choses si équivoques, et de si peu de conséquence, qu'elles se désavouent sur-le-champ' (p.76).

So it is that Madame de Lursay is obliged to teach her pupil the importance of *gradations*: 'je mettais chaque précepte en pratique à mesure qu'elle me le donnait, et l'étude importante des gradations aurait pu nous mener fort loin, si nous n'eussions entendu dans l'antichambre, un bruit qui nous força de l'interrompre' (p.142). Nevertheless, despite the interruption on the occasion of that tête-à-tête, Meilcour is finally able to put to good effect the lesson learned on the day that she taught him 'par quelles progressions on arrive aux plaisirs, et combien l'amour les subdivise' (p.245).

Meilcour's successful initiation, both sexually and in the world of manners, comes at the end of a scene that begins with him intending to punish her for having deceived him with an appearance of respectability. Madame de Lursay rapidly turns the tables, the accuser becomes the accused and the lady enquires: 'N'était-ce pas à vous à connaître, et saisir mes mouvements?' (p.236). Even more illustrative of the social code that governs the relations of men and women and that he has failed to observe, in the same scene she taunts him with the biting comment, '...si je puis vous le dire, c'est à vous, et non à moi, qu'il a plu de faire une belle résistance' (p.239). The final irony, as Brooks remarks, is that 'superior worldliness leads to the same *dénouement*, if not by the same routes' (*15*, p.31). If he had known the code, Meilcour would have succeeded with Madame de Lursay much more rapidly. He had merely delayed the inevitable through his ignorance.

Crébillon has confronted Meilcour with three carefully chosen types of feminine character on his entry into the world. The first is Madame de Lursay, the *femme de tête*; the second is Madame de Senanges, the libertine; the third is Hortense de Théville, the young girl making her own entry into society. All are portraits representative of women of that period in a particular social class.

As the story is told by the memorialist, the relationship between Meilcour and Madame de Lursay is the most obvious and clearly defined. She may be seen as an experienced predator who, by means of calculated moves, attracts, then loses Meilcour, regains control over him and achieves his submission to her will. It can easily be perceived that the structure of the novel lies precisely in that movement in the young Meilcour's thoughts and feelings that draws him towards Madame de Lursay, then away from her, only to return to her in the final sequence.

Conroy points to the nostalgic view taken by the older narrator that gives to Madame de Lursay a prominent position, when he writes 'in one sense Meilcour offers as homage to Madame de Lursay his *mémoires*, a testimony to the importance she has for him.

Essentially (and especially from Meilcour's point of view) Madame de Lursay is the principal character; she is the most sympathetic and the most intelligent personage in the novel. ... By telling her story, by focusing his attention, and therefore the reader's, on Madame de Lursay in preference to other stories which are implicitly contained in the givens of this novel, Meilcour is making a choice which is pregnant with meaning' (*18*, p.103).

The portrait that Meilcour provides by way of introduction to Madame de Lursay has the classical balance of the genre, but nevertheless is much more flattering than critical. He begins with her outward appearance and comments that, as a mature woman, she had retained her beauty: 'Elle était belle, mais d'une beauté majestueuse. ... Elle était grande et bien faite; et, dans sa nonchalance affectée, peu de femmes avaient autant de grâces qu'elle. Sa physionomie et ses yeux étaient sévères forcément; et lorsqu'elle ne songeait pas à s'observer on y voyait briller l'enjouement et la tendresse' (p.74).

When he proceeds to describe her moral qualities, Meilcour is equally positive: 'Elle avait l'esprit vif, mais sans étourderie, prudent, même dissimulé. Elle parlait bien, et parlait aisément; avec beaucoup de finesse dans les pensées, elle n'était pas précieuse. Elle avait étudié avec soin son sexe et le nôtre, et connaissait tous les ressorts qui les font agir' (p.74). As Dagen comments in a note (*14*, p.251, n.19), this suggests an awareness by the older Meilcour of the existence of a science of behaviour or worldliness that Madame de Lursay is later depicted as putting into effect. 'Au reste, quoique prude, elle était douce dans la société. Son système n'était point, qu'on ne dût pas avoir des faiblesses, mais que le sentiment seul pouvait les rendre pardonnables...' (p.74). So it is that, as Meilcour remarks, 'elle voulait, s'il était possible, que ma tendresse pour elle ne fût pas une affaire de peu de jours; et, moins aimé, j'aurais trouvé moins de résistance' (p.85). This may also explain her *cri de cœur* before she gives herself to Meilcour in the final scene: '...et je suis perdue, si je ne suis pas heureuse' (p.245). In keeping with the mood of the age, Madame de Lursay is typically a character both of sensuality and also of observance of a code of behaviour after careful study of the motivations of both sexes.

The importance of *sentiment*, feeling as a justification for human weaknesses of the flesh, is advanced at the conclusion of Meilcour's portrait of Madame de Lursay. By contrast, there are those women without feeling, worthy of contempt in their dishonourable conduct. Such is the libertine Madame de Senanges, a feminine version of Versac without his intelligence and lucidity, seeking avidly the gratification of the senses and the corruption of others, unconcerned about what society thinks of her behaviour.

Her portrait, when later she appears on the scene (pp.145-46), is markedly in contrast with that of Madame de Lursay. It begins with the remark that Meilcour was to have the misfortune to owe his education to this woman and he makes a number of derogatory judgments about her before describing her appearance. Madame de Lursay was anxious to conserve her reputation in the eyes of society, but Madame de Senanges 'était une de ces femmes philosophes' (see Dagen's explanatory note to the effect that this hedonistic philosophy enabled such women to despise public opinion and to reject the illusions of the heart; p.255, n. 59). This type of woman, whose cynicism authorises hedonism, is to be found frequently in Crébillon's work. A series of contrasting attitudes amplifies what is meant by this 'philosophy': 's'excusant toujours sur un premier mouvement, dont elles n'ont jamais senti la puissance, et qu'elles veulent trouver partout; sans caractère comme sans passions; faibles sans être sensibles; cédant sans cesse à l'idée d'un plaisir qui les fuit toujours...' (p.145). These generalisations condemn a whole group of society women, typified by Madame de Senanges, 'telles, en un mot, qu'on ne peut jamais ni les excuser, ni les plaindre' (ibid.).

When Meilcour turns his attention to her outward appearance, the portrait is scathing: 'Le fard qui achevait de flétrir les tristes restes de sa beauté, sa parure outrée, son maintien immodeste, ne la rendait que moins supportable' (ibid.). He paints 'un tableau de corruption, qu'on ne peut regarder sans horreur' (p.146).

As to the qualities of mind of Madame de Senanges, she possesses wit such as is commonly found in society: Crébillon will later illustrate this in practice in scenes of dialogue and it will form part of Versac's lesson to the young Meilcour. She gossips avidly, disparages everyone and speaks her mind to the detriment of all without concern for her own ignorance of any topic of conversation. She expresses herself in the slang fashionable at Court, with the languid accent of the 'extrêmement bonne compagnie'.

This is an exclusive and limited circle of the aristocracy and includes the character Versac, who plays an important role in the text and becomes the prototype for the innumerable *petits-maîtres* in the novels that follow in the course of the century. The portrait of Versac appears when he pays a visit to Madame de Meilcour (pp.129-30), who dislikes him, doubtless fearing his influence on her son.

It is clear that he is admired by Meilcour, who begins by stating that Versac will have an important role to play in the development of his memoirs. He attributes to Versac 'la plus haute naissance, l'esprit le plus agréable, et la figure la plus séduisante'. There follows a series of characteristics and behaviour that the reader may not consider particularly flattering, but the subject of the portrait has obviously captivated Meilcour and many others:

> Adoré de toutes les femmes, qu'il trompait et déchirait sans cesse, vain, impérieux, étourdi, le plus audacieux petit-maître qu'on eût jamais vu, et plus cher peut-être à leurs yeux par ces mêmes défauts, quelque contraires qu'ils leur soient: quoiqu'il en puisse être, elles l'avaient mis à la mode, dès l'instant qu'il était entré dans le monde, et il était depuis dix ans en possession de vaincre les plus insensibles, de fixer les plus coquettes, et de déplacer les amants les plus accrédités; ou s'il lui était arrivé de ne pas réussir, il avait toujours su tourner les choses si bien à son avantage, que la Dame n'en passait pas moins pour lui avoir appartenu.

Versac will then be shown in action in society directly after his portrait is concluded, displaying his varied talents before Madame de Meilcour, then at the 'scène du souper' and in the promenades of the Tuileries gardens, and it is he who will give to Meilcour the lesson about society and its code that will eventually permit the young initiate to reach the point that he mentions at the end of the portrait: 'moi-même, qui ai depuis marché si avantageusement sur ses traces, et qui parvins enfin à mettre la Cour et Paris entre nous deux...' The impressions of the young Meilcour and of the older narrator are mingled here, as indicated by the change of tense at the conclusion of the portrait.

Versac's superiority in his genre is emphasised when he is accompanied by Pranzi, 'homme à la mode, élève et copie éternelle de Versac' (p.147), since Versac is inimitable. The portrait given (p.149) is unequivocally pejorative. Pranzi talks incessantly of his lineage, even though his family is only recently ennobled. He has ceased to boast of his courage after certain unfortunate experiences. 'Né sans esprit, comme sans agréments, sans figure, sans bien, le caprice des femmes et la protection de Versac en avaient fait un homme à bonnes fortunes, quoiqu'il joignît à ses autres défauts le vice bas de dépouiller celles à qui il inspirait du goût' (p.149). A string of further unpleasant characteristics concludes the portrait: 'Sot, présomptueux, impudent, aussi incapable de bien penser, que de rougir de penser mal; s'il n'avait pas été un fat, ... on n'aurait jamais su ce qui pouvait lui donner le droit de plaire' (ibid.). And indeed, Meilcour and the reader are amazed to discover that Pranzi had been closely involved with Madame de Lursay ten years earlier.

These portraits of the *femme de tête*, the female libertine, the petit-maître and the *fat* were clearly typical of a certain section of contemporary society. Crébillon was praised for his acute portrayal of a period, a social world and social relations that he had observed; there is stylisation, but also accuracy of description and analysis in the neo-classical French mode. Whether Crébillon was fascinated or repulsed by the *extrêmement bonne compagnie*, and indeed the format of the memoir permits him to take refuge behind the naivety of the young Meilcour and the cynicism of the elder memorialist, there remains an ambiguity, an amorality in the author's view of the behaviour of Meilcour and his contemporaries.

To complete the feminine portraits, Crébillon introduces the young girl Hortense, entering a society that must be as bewildering to her as to Meilcour. The description given by the young man at the Opera is a reminiscence of the superlatives typically employed in the novels of sensibility of the period: 'Qu'on se figure tout ce que la beauté la plus régulière a de plus noble, tout ce que les grâces ont de plus séduisant, en un mot, tout ce que la jeunesse peut répandre de fraîcheur et d'éclat, à peine pourra-t-on se faire une idée de la

personne que je voudrais dépeindre' (pp.89-90). Crébillon has
recourse to the tradition of the *coup de foudre*, as in Prévost's
Manon Lescaut: 'j'y portai mes regards; et l'objet qui s'y offrit les
fixa'. Indeed, Crébillon emphasises that it is 'un de ces coups de
surprise qui caractérisent dans les romans les grandes aventures'
(p.92). There is also a reference to a contemporary novel, *La Vie de
Marianne* by Marivaux, when Meilcour wonders how to engage in
conversation the object of his love and thinks of Marianne spraining
her ankle and being assisted by Valville, who is then able to press his
suit with her (p.111).

This relationship is the only one in the text that justifies
Crébillon's comment in the Preface that 'l'amour seul préside ici; ou,
si, de temps en temps, quelque autre motif s'y joint, c'est presque
toujours lui qui le détermine' (p.68). We return here to the theme of
ambiguity, for a relationship with Hortense is always portrayed as a
dream on Meilcour's part. His mother refuses to contemplate any
prospect of marriage with her and in any case he is constantly torn
between his desire for Madame de Lursay and his feelings for
Hortense, leading to *égarements* of the heart and the mind, as
indicated in the title, and which remain unresolved.

Crébillon admired as novelists Prévost, Marivaux and Mme de
Graffigny, while rejecting the *roman d'aventure* which he satirises in
his Preface and within the text. However, he invents a genre that is
original, the psychological novel of the metaphysics of sentiment.
Meilcour may feel *amour de cœur* or *tendresse* for Hortense, but it is
amour-goût that he feels for Madame de Lursay and, as Versac tells
him in regard to Madame de Senanges and what she expects of him,
'Votre cœur! ... jargon de roman... C'est, en un mot, du goût qu'elle
a pour vous, et ce n'est que du goût que vous lui devez' (p.207).
Versac even gives his pupil a definition of *amour-goût*: 'Une sorte
de commerce intime... une amitié vive qui ressemble à l'amour par
les plaisirs, sans en avoir les sottes délicatesses' (ibid.).

While certain writers, such as Diderot, distanced themselves
from Crébillon because of his perceived eroticism, in fact his
concern is with an analysis of the subtleties of such distinctions as
amour-goût and its effect on human relationships within society.

Crébillon plays an essential role in establishing distinctions of
vocabulary that differentiate between feelings. He places Madame de

Senanges, who seeks merely to 'please' rather than to 'affect emotionally', and who was 'très persuadée que ses charmes agissaient sur moi comme il lui convenait' (p.147) at her first meeting with Meilcour, in contrast with Madame de Lursay, who 'en disant qu'elle ne cherchait pas à plaire, ... se mettait toujours en état de toucher' (p.74). Thus, for Madame de Lursay, 'le sentiment seul' (ibid.) excused weakness; she is 'sensible' but also 'délicate'.

The feelings of love, whether of *tendresse* or *sensibilité* or *désir* expressed as *goût*, are involuntary and a matter of surprise. Meilcour experiences the *coup de foudre* for Hortense at the Opera and he feels a caprice for Madame de Lursay, but he lacks experience to take advantage of the moment or occasion with a woman only too willing to encourage him in his enterprise: 'Le feu que je voyais dans ses yeux, et qui aurait été pour tout autre un coup de lumière, son trouble, l'altération de sa voix, ses soupirs doux et fréquents, tout ajoutait à l'occasion, et rien ne me la fit comprendre' (pp.126-27).

Madame de Lursay leads Meilcour to forsake the feelings of the heart, *tendresse*, in favour of *goût*, to a great extent from vanity; Versac tries to persuade Meilcour that love does not exist and encourages him strongly to seek the publicity of an affair with Madame de Senanges. In fact, the relationship with Madame de Lursay is not an *égarement du cœur*, it is rather a *caprice de tête* because Meilcour feels only for Hortense with his heart. Crébillon suggests, however, that Meilcour will move on to Madame de Senanges, for whom initially he feels nothing but disgust. Even with Madame de Lursay, at the moment of her capitulation, the elder Meilcour writes: 'L'ouvrage de mes sens me parut celui de mon cœur' (p.245). In the case of Madame de Senanges, his imagination, totally confused, will make him believe that he feels, and both head and heart will be disorientated.

In the text as we have it, Meilcour is not yet aware of that '*quiétisme de l'amour*' (p.248) that would have permitted him, in the arms of Madame de Lursay, to take advantage of 'tous les charmes de l'occasion' without running the risk of being unfaithful to Hortense. Such are the metaphysics of sentiment within a code of worldliness, as expressed by the memorialist recounting his experience of love as he had known it. It may be felt that the remark he makes to Versac is almost a premonition: 'Il me semble que ce n'est pas travailler pour ses plaisirs, que de chercher tant à connaître les femmes. Cette étude, quand on ne la perd pas de vue, occupe l'esprit dans les temps mêmes où le sentiment seul devrait agir' (p.222). This comment precedes Meilcour's first sexual experience and anticipates his disillusion.

3. Social Realism and Satire

There is social realism in the text of *Les Egarements*, as has already been established in the previous chapter. The codes of *libertinage* and worldliness required by a *salon* society where everyone is under observation are minutely analysed by Crébillon. His character Versac has the function of explaining the code of *libertinage*, Madame de Lursay that of worldliness.

The text depicts in action, particularly through dialogue, a series of types, both masculine and feminine, who exemplify a small but influential section of French society at a specific period under the *ancien régime*. The influence may be seen of the moralist La Bruyère and his *Caractères* (1688). The realism and accuracy of the portrayal of these types, as confirmed by contemporaries, is fundamental to the success of a plot that would otherwise be much less entertaining to the reader.

'Présenter aux hommes la peinture de leurs vices, de leurs travers et de leurs ridicules, les aider à se mieux connaître, se mieux comprendre, et par cela même les aider peut-être à se réformer, tout en les amusant. Tel est brièvement le but que se propose Crébillon ...' (*34*, p.157). Crébillon's intentions are indeed made clear in his Preface to the text of *Les Egarements*. He believes in the Classical precept that the aim of the artist is both to instruct and entertain and he will do this through the novel form with realism of psychology and social setting, 'le tableau de la vie humaine' (p.65). The portraits of the characters are described as Meilcour saw them at the time, influenced in his commentary by his later experience of society. They have their virtues and their vices, their ridiculous aspects worthy of satire. This creates the realistic element of the description, a universal truth applicable to that social setting and to many others, 'Le vrai seul subsiste toujours' (p.66).

Crébillon warns the reader in his Preface against seeing in *Les Egarements* a *roman à clé*. His characters have attributes applicable to living persons, among them *petits-maîtres* and prudes, and his portraits are to be found 'dans le sein de la Nature' (p.66) rather than in a particular individual.

The art of Crébillon is to describe a section of society through the eyes of a young man who is ignorant as yet of that society in which he will be obliged to play a role. The reader will develop a knowledge of the adolescent Meilcour as he experiences his first liaison, with the addition of the reflections of the mature Meilcour on this first adventure, and the lessons offered by it, the element of instruction. Versac, astonished by the adolescent's naivety, brings his own experience to a judgment of women and society with a harshness that displays his own cynicism and revolt and attributes his own vices, for the benefit of Meilcour and the reader, to the society that has formed him. His social criticism is nonetheless well-founded and he acts as Crébillon's spokesman.

As evidenced by his Preface, Crébillon, like his contemporaries, was ever preoccupied with the ethical dimension of his literary work. In the eighteenth century, readers were apt to stress the moral or, as they saw it, the immoral aspect of the novel, in particular if it were by Crébillon. The lesson given by Versac without contradiction from any other major character, and his central place in the novel as Crébillon's apparent spokesman, added weight to accusations that the author approved of, or at least refused to condemn a frivolous society of libertines. The portraits of other characters, whether prude or female libertine, do not change this viewpoint.

Social realism can easily be read as satire according to the taste and turn of mind of the reader. Within the overall realistic setting that Crébillon describes, there certainly exist specific elements of satire. Meilcour himself, in his adolescent state, can be seen as a target for satire, his naivety providing numerous opportunities for comic effects. Dagen notes a comment by Madame de Lursay to Meilcour:

> ... nous sommes seules, vous me dites que vous m'aimez, je vous réponds que je vous aime, rien ne nous gêne: plus la liberté que je semble donner à vos désirs, est grande, plus vous êtes estimable de ne point chercher à en abuser. Vous êtes peut-être le seul au monde que je connaisse capable de ce procédé. Aussi la répugnance,

que je me suis toujours sentie pour ce que je fais
aujourd'hui cesse-t-elle. Je puis me flatter enfin d'avoir
trouvé un cœur dans les principes du mien. (p.126)

This can be described as sarcastic, even malicious: 'Pour ne voir là
aucun malice, faut-il que le naïf amant soit égaré!' (*19*, p.82).

Crébillon stresses the comic behaviour of his hero paralysed by
timidity and unable to take advantage of social opportunities with
women. An obvious example of this in the development of his
relationship with Madame de Lursay occurs when she arranges for
the two of them to be alone. The story is of course told by Meilcour.
'Ce moment si ardemment souhaité vint enfin ...' but 'Je ne me vis
pas plutôt seul avec elle, que je fus saisi de la plus horrible peur que
j'aie eue de ma vie. Je ne saurais exprimer la révolution qui se fit
dans tous mes sens. Je tremblais, j'étais interdit. Je n'osais regarder
Madame de Lursay...' (p.121). She waits for him to speak and when
he does so, it is to state: 'Vous faites donc des nœuds, Madame? lui
demandai-je d'une voix tremblante'. In this instance, the adolescent
Meilcour hardly needs the experience of his mature self to laugh at
his own behaviour and his meaningless comment on her futile
pastime. 'A cette intéressante et spirituelle question, Madame de
Lursay me regarda avec étonnement. Quelque idée qu'elle se fût
faite de ma timidité, et du peu d'usage que j'avais du monde, il lui
parut inconcevable que je ne trouvasse que cela à lui dire' (p.122).

Meilcour fares no better with Hortense de Théville in attracting
her favourable attention towards him. When he sets out to intercept
Hortense walking in the Tuileries gardens in company with an
unknown lady, following the conversation between them that he has
overheard, it is timidity that overcomes him: 'mais, timide comme je
l'étais, je tremblais de me présenter à ses yeux... Mon émotion
redoubla. Je profitai de l'espace qui était encore entre nous deux
pour la regarder avec toute la tendresse qu'elle m'inspirait: à mesure
qu'elle s'avançait vers moi, je sentais mon trouble s'augmenter, et
ma timidité renaître' (p.110). In a crushing anticlimax, Meilcour
finds to his chagrin that Hortense has not even noticed him and his
vanity is hurt. Crébillon stresses vanity as a central element of his
character, applying the same characteristic to other characters, such

as Versac and Pranzi. No doubt seeing it as an innate vice of human nature, worthy of satire, and at the least applicable to the *petit-maître*, he ascribes to Meilcour the reflection 'j'avais sans doute dans le cœur le germe de ce que j'ai été depuis ... ne pouvant penser mal longtemps de moi-même, je m'imaginai que la modestie seule l'avait contrainte à ce qu'elle venait de faire' (p.111).

Meilcour convinces himself that Hortense could not have failed to notice him and again sets out to intercept the two ladies. This time, he obtains for his pains a brief curtsey from Hortense, who keeps her eyes lowered, not even meeting his admiring gaze. Crébillon concludes this scene of mortification of his young hero with a further reflection that indicates, in a comic manner, the distance between the unreal world of coincidence to be found in novels and the reality of human experience. 'Je me rappelai alors toutes les occasions que j'avais lues dans les romans de parler à sa maîtresse, et je fus surpris qu'il n'y en eût pas une dont je pusse faire usage. Je souhaitai mille fois qu'elle fît un faux pas, qu'elle se donnât même une entorse: je ne voyais plus que ce moyen pour engager la conversation; mais il me manqua encore, et je la vis monter en carrosse, sans qu'il lui arrivât d'accident dont je pusse tirer avantage' (p.111). Crébillon refuses to bring coincidence to Meilcour's aid, shows him as passively and foolishly taking refuge in a dream-world of illusion, and suggests that in contrast his own novel is grounded in social realism, while Marivaux's heroine Marianne is enabled to meet Valville and develop their relationship only through authorial trickery.

Within this overall realistic setting, however, there are specific elements of satire directed at the representative types making up the social group. This cast of players is small. Certain minor characters, such as Madame de Meilcour, Madame de Théville and the unknown lady accompanying Hortense on her walk in the Tuileries gardens, express moral sentiments presumably intended to contribute to the education of Meilcour and any other listeners. Madame de Meilcour is praised by her son for the education she gave him, even though she makes it clear to him that she does not believe in the lasting effects of the *coup de foudre* and that she has other plans for his future than marriage to Hortense. Madame de Théville is portrayed as a lady of strict morality, somewhat abrasive in personal relations and, as

Meilcour comments rather mischievously, characterised as a person 'qui aimait le jeu, comme une femme qui n'aime point autre chose' (p.160). The lady overheard in the Tuileries gardens gives advice to Hortense on love and relations with men that Meilcour could equally have taken to heart.

There are other more central characters that express a different viewpoint, such as Madame de Lursay, Madame de Senanges, Madame de Mongennes, Versac and Pranzi and these constitute, to a greater or lesser degree, the targets for Crébillon's satire of prevailing vices or follies. There are distinctions that must be made, since criticism, or implied criticism, is not true satire. Madame de Lursay, seen favourably through the eyes of Meilcour, is shown to be a woman of feeling who believes that genuine sentiment justifies relationships with the men she has chosen and, as Meilcour states, he would have had less difficulty in overcoming any resistance on her part if it were not for her desire for mutual commitment. Her way of thought is described as a system and her philosophy that of Plato. Meilcour's comment is that it is a 'sorte de discours rabattu, que tiennent sans cesse les trois quarts des femmes, et qui ne rendent que plus méprisables celles qui le déshonorent par leur conduite' (p.74). This suggests that the mature Meilcour disputes the logic of the argument, which is used by so many women to justify immoral conduct, but his criticism is not directed at Madame de Lursay, for if she did not possess 'toutes les vertus de son sexe, elle en avait du moins; ses faiblesses étaient cachées sous des dehors imposants, elle pensait et s'exprimait avec noblesse...' (p.183).

In contrast, the most obvious feminine target for satire is Madame de Senanges. Meilcour portrays her as ageing and unattractive, but totally oblivious to the impression she makes on others because of the high opinion she has of herself. Madame de Senanges is persuaded that Meilcour was attracted to her from the first, disregarding any appearance to the contrary. It is a comment on the decadence of that society when Versac insists to Meilcour that he has no choice but to submit to a liaison with Madame de Senanges; even more so that Meilcour admits he later became involved with her despite his initial repugnance, expressed in the strongest possible terms:

> Faite pour le mépris, il semblait qu'elle craignît qu'on ne
> vît pas assez tôt combien on lui en devait: ses idées
> étaient puériles, et ses discours rebutants. Jamais elle
> n'avait su masquer ses vues, et l'on ne saurait dire ce
> qu'elle paraissait dans les cas où presque toutes les
> femmes de son espèce ont l'art de ne passer que pour
> galantes. Quelquefois cependant elle prenait des tons de
> dignité, mais qui la rendaient si ridicule: elle soutenait si
> mal l'air d'une personne respectable, que l'on ne voyait
> jamais mieux à quel point la vertu lui était étrangère, que
> quand elle feignait de la connaître. (p.183)

Indeed, Meilcour specifically attacks the manner in which she boasts of her social position and yet behaves so reprehensively, without any attempt to conceal her dissolute conduct.

Madame de Mongennes appears only briefly in the text, when Meilcour finds himself obliged to accompany the two ladies on their walk in the Tuileries gardens, and he is the object of desire of them both, without having the least interest in either. As Meilcour declares, 'Madame de Mongennes, surtout, me déplaisait' (p.185), and he proceeds to give a very unflattering portrait of her, even though she has the advantage of youth over her companion Madame de Senanges. He concludes: 'Telle qu'elle était cependant, elle plaisait, et ses vices lui tenaient lieu d'agréments dans un siècle où, pour être de mode, une femme ne pouvait trop marquer jusqu'où elle portait l'extravagance et le dérèglement' (ibid.). Madame de Mongennes therefore also becomes representative of the decadence of the period, observing the maxim that, for a woman, too easy a virtue and too great severity of virtue are equally to be feared. This leads her to a pretence of lack of interest in Meilcour, followed an hour later by obvious signs of attraction to him, since she, too, is persuaded by her own misplaced self-esteem that Meilcour will give her the preference.

Versac is admired by Meilcour and the reader sees him as represented by the young man who wishes only to emulate him, despite being forbidden to see him by his mother. From the initial portrait, the reader learns that women have placed Versac in his socially dominant position and that he responds by attacking them at every opportunity, 'adoré de toutes les femmes, qu'il trompait et déchirait sans cesse...' (p.129). Versac is a product of the French *salon*, where women, from the early seventeenth century onwards, had a beneficial, civilising influence on men, but where equally there existed a type epitomised by Versac, who was resentful of the control exercised over him by women and set out to make them pay by their loss of reputation and disgrace for the thwarting of his own ambitions, which might well have merited a much wider sphere of influence in a different and less confined society.

Meilcour portrays Versac as irresistible to women and Versac has the pretention to share this opinion. He has no doubt of his ability to seduce Hortense, despite the warnings she had been given against him. However, 'il s'aperçut bientôt qu'elle était insensible aux agaceries des yeux, et qu'elle n'avait pas été étonnée de sa figure: cela le surprit' (p.150). Not to be easily dissuaded, Versac 'étala ses charmes: il avait la jambe belle, il la fit valoir; il rit le plus souvent qu'il put, pour montrer ses dents, il prit enfin les contenances les plus décisives, celles qui montrent le mieux la taille, et en développent le plus les grâces' (p.151). In fact, Meilcour's admiration cannot save Versac from appearing ridiculous in this scene and he has no more success with Hortense than his pupil.

It is in his instruction of Meilcour during their walk together at the Etoile that Versac expresses himself frankly on the subject of worldly success. Meilcour must become an actor, observing and learning the rules of worldly behaviour, particularly the *ridicules en crédit*. While the conventions of fashion must be followed, new *ridicules* should constantly be invented by the *petit-maître*, who satisfies his vanity and sense of superiority by leading the fashionable world of women in their pastimes. Morality is to be replaced by the follies that are acceptable, despite Meilcour's objection that he cannot see himself adopting 'un système qui m'obligerait à cacher les vertus que je puis avoir, pour me parer des vices que je n'aurais pas' (p.217). The fact that Meilcour keeps Versac's secret that he is capable of thought and undertakes a career in which he will 'prendre les erreurs de son siècle, ou du moins s'y plier' (p.218) is illustrative of Crébillon's implicit criticism of the society controlled by these *petits-maîtres*.

Pranzi has a limited role to play in relation to Versac, rather as Madame de Mongennes complements Madame de Senanges. He emulates Versac without ever succeeding in his aim and the wonder is that he is acceptable in society and that he has been favoured by Madame de Lursay in the past. He talks ceaselessly and without justification of his noble lineage and exaggerates his courage until he pays the price. Pranzi relies on the protection of Versac and represents a type that Crébillon clearly thought to be without redeeming features, but who nevertheless was an accepted *habitué* of *salon* society.

Meilcour, in telling the story of his education, never expresses any morality based on orthodox Catholic religious tenets, nor is the religious viewpoint brought out through other characters. In his introduction, Meilcour merely contrasts what he has read of feminine behaviour in *anciens mémoires*, presumably relating to courtly love in the medieval period, with what he sees around him in a decadent society, but he gives no specific basis for an acceptable morality, which would contrast with behaviour worthy of satire. Nor is political satire to be found in *Les Egarements*.

4. The World of Illusion

The theme of illusion is central to *Les Egarements du cœur et de l'esprit* because the first-person narrative allows Crébillon to show how Meilcour deceives himself about society and also about his own feelings. The older Meilcour cynically comments on his own behaviour, thoughts and feelings upon his entry into the world and brings out clearly his own disillusion, on the basis of his acquired experience of society, for the benefit of the reader, expressing as he does so the theme of a sentimental education.

That theme will of course be further developed later in novels that are acknowledged classics of European literature, such as Goethe's four-volume novel *Wilhelm Meisters Lehrjahre* (1795-96), in which his hero, from a middle-class background, encounters life at different levels of society, and experiences a number of love relationships that are central to his development and constitute his sentimental education. Then Flaubert, in the second half of the nineteenth century, develops the theme in great depth, including his perception of his own generation, that of the failed revolution of 1848, which he associates with the anti-hero's failure in his love-affairs.

In his memoirs, Meilcour introduces himself as having 'l'imagination ardente, et facile à se laisser frapper' (p.70). He seeks to banish his 'ennui intérieur', so common at the period, by engaging in a love-affair: 'je ne songeai plus qu'à me faire une passion, telle qu'elle pût être'. The memoirs of Marianne also will be fixed on thoughts of love, in her case complicated by the need for social advancement. But their voyages of discovery will be very different.

Marianne, in her reflections, subtly distinguishes between her stated intentions and certain other motives and pretexts that remain unformulated and constitute perhaps the real motivation for her behaviour. This reminds us of the pessimism of the seventeenth-century classical moralists, with their belief in self-interest as the key to motivation, but while Marivaux regards his heroine's reflections as a lesson in helping to attain a personal morality, Crébillon assumes an egotistic, vicious human nature and depicts Meilcour as becoming gradually disillusioned about love, sincerity and the permanence of relationships. The scepticism of Crébillon based on rationalism has an entirely different spirit from the faith placed by Marivaux, not only in reason but also in sentiment.

Prévost's Chevalier des Grieux believes in passion as a virtue in itself. In telling his story, which begins when he experiences the *coup de foudre* for Manon, he sees himself as bound by sentiment, destined to follow Manon wherever she may lead, and indeed he is freed to return to his former life only by her death. There is no rationalism in this view, the intelligence is entirely subjugated by the heart and the equation of heart and mind does not exist.

In Crébillon's world, imagination, dreams and reverie are not absent from the text, but form part of the theme of illusion. Meilcour spends three sleepless nights: the first is spent 'tantôt à rêver aux moyens de rendre Madame de Lursay sensible, tantôt à m'encourager à ne plus penser à elle' (p.86); the second sleepless night, the culmination of the following day, when he tries unsuccessfully to think of another object for his affections apart from Madame de Lursay, 'j'employai presque toute la nuit à repasser dans mon esprit les femmes auxquelles je pouvais m'attacher' (p.88); the third occurs after the scene in the Tuileries gardens, 'je passai toute la nuit à faire sur mon aventure les plus cruelles, et les plus inutiles réflexions' (p.202). This last comment is followed by the generalisation, presumably applicable to Meilcour: 'On connaît assez les songes des amants, leurs incertitudes, leurs différentes résolutions' (ibid.) and indeed this has proved to be characteristic of Meilcour's imaginings, which retain him within a circle of passivity in which his lack of experience prevents him from taking an active, decisive posture in pursuit of the object, or objects, of his love. He imagines that he knows whom or what he wants, but he remains unsure of his own feelings and how to act in his own interests, so can easily be *égaré*, that is misled, by others.

The form of the memoir-novel authorises Crébillon to superimpose changes of time and point of view. The author mingles the opinions of the young hero and of the narrator, including other periods of the lives of Meilcour, of Madame de Lursay, of Versac;

only the viewpoint of Hortense remains unknown, as opaque to the reader as to Meilcour. The changes in point of view are discussed by William Edmiston in his article on the subject of 'Selective focalization and *égarement*' in Crébillon's novel, to which reference has already been made (see above pp.15-16). He points out that the memoir form involves the use by the narrator of changes of tense for specific purposes.

The present tense can indicate a shared viewpoint on the part of the older narrator, his younger self and a contemporary reader of this novel of worldliness. From his introductory comments in setting the scene, the narrator uses the present tense in a generalised sense of wide applicability within a particular social group. 'J'entrai dans le monde à dix-sept ans, et avec tous les avantages qui peuvent y faire remarquer' (p.69). In describing his way of thought as an adolescent, he continues, 'il est ordinaire, lorsque l'on pense ainsi, de s'estimer plus qu'on ne vaut' (ibid.). He provides an explanation for his concentration on pleasure to be found through women, 'le peu d'occupation, que se font communément les gens de mon rang et de mon âge' (ibid.). He makes a general observation on the reasons for his initial choice of conquest: 'On s'attache souvent moins à la femme qui touche le plus, qu'à celle qu'on croit le plus facilement toucher' (p.70). He introduces his commentary on the society of his time by reference to a previous age with stricter moral standards, 'si nous en croyons d'anciens Mémoires' (p.71). He vouches for the truth of his remarks on contemporary society: 'Nous croyons difficilement, que des vices et des vertus qui ne sont plus sous nos yeux, aient jamais existé: il est cependant réel que je n'exagère pas' (p.72).

The narrator also emphasises his involvement in the introduction by bringing to the story his experience of the behaviour of women. With regard to Mme de Meilcour, he stresses her selflessness in favour of her son's education: 'Ce projet, je crois, serait entré dans l'esprit de peu de femmes' (p.69). When he refers to other women, his experience is even more emphatic, since 'je suis même certain que quand je les aurais mieux connues, je n'en aurais pas été moins timide' (p.72).

Meilcour as narrator changes tense within his introduction to indicate information that he has obtained since the time of the events he is about to recount. 'Mais, Madame de Meilcour, qui, à ce que l'on m'a dit, n'avait point été coquette dans sa jeunesse, et que je n'ai pas vue galante sur son retour' (p.69). In making a comparison between himself and his younger self, he tells the reader that his mother's concern for his education had not succeeded in making him less proud and self-satisfied, but at least he had been obliged to conceal these vices that would have developed even more as a feature of his character without her efforts. He is also in a position to tell the reader that behaviour in society had become very different by the time he was writing his memoirs than at the time of the events described.

All of this makes interpretation of character difficult, because the psychology of Meilcour is essentially multi-faceted. On the one hand, the memorialist has knowledge of thoughts, feelings and intentions that would have been impossible for him to know. This is a matter of the technique of novel-writing and is more apparent to the modern reader than to Crébillon's contemporaries. It results in greater importance being given to the older narrator, who possesses the wider knowledge that he would be expected to have, and even knowledge beyond that. On the other hand, there is a vacuity, an emptiness at the centre of Meilcour because, as a young man, he did not know his own personality or what morality he was intended to live by or would choose to live by. Hence an ambiguity of character and of morality, an irony highly appreciated in the eighteenth century and emphasised by the dichotomy between the naive adolescent Meilcour and the cynical narrator, able to comment from his own libertine perspective.

Such false precepts as Meilcour learns are counterbalanced by his passion for Hortense, but the world she represents, with its accent on fidelity and opposition to *libertinage*, presents too many obstacles: 'Pensez-vous donc, me demanda-t-elle, qu'il suffise d'être aimé pour être heureux, et qu'une passion mutuelle ne soit pas le comble du malheur, lorsque tout s'oppose à sa félicité?' (p.173). The ambiguity of Meilcour's morality would have been condemned by the Catholic Church and the establishment, but an age devoted to the *chasse au plaisir* accepted such ambiguity unconcernedly, indeed relished Crébillon's exploitation of it.

It is Versac who gives Meilcour his lesson in worldly manners. He introduces the initiate to the philosophic stage of his formation, in the sense that the eighteenth century sometimes used the term 'philosophy' (see Dagen's note 118, p.260: the *philosophe* in this text is 'un homme qui par libertinage se met au-dessus des devoirs et obligations').

What Versac also reveals is an ambiguity within himself: 'Je me flatte, au reste, que vous saurez me garder le secret le plus inviolable sur ce que je vous dis, et sur ce que je vais vous dire. Quoi! lui dis-je en riant, vous pourriez être fâché que je disse, *Versac sait penser*' (p.209). The lesson imparted is a secret and the methods of worldly success that Versac reveals are illustrative of a man who has purposely deformed himself to achieve that success: 'Pensez-vous que je me sois condamné sans réflexion au tourment de me déguiser sans cesse? ... je me créai les vices dont j'avais besoin pour plaire... Je suis né si différent de ce que je parais, que ce ne fut pas sans une peine extrême, que je parvins à me gâter l'esprit' (p.214). It is to be presumed that Versac retains his prestige in Meilcour's eyes after he has purposely removed his mask during this long conversation, for the reader knows that Meilcour will follow in Versac's path to become an accomplished libertine. However, the interpretation of Versac's character, aided by these revelations, is still difficult to determine. He sees himself without illusion, there is a contempt of self, and hatred for a society that reduces a man of talent to such futilities: his cynicism separates him from others and his solitary misfortune is part of a universal malady within his caste. Versac may be seen as both the idol and the victim of society.

The lesson that Versac gives to Meilcour takes up some sixteen pages of the text (pp.207-23) and could be seen as an interruption of the story told by the memorialist, but since its function within the structure of the text is to initiate and to destroy illusions about society, it is clearly central to the psychological theme. The novel is concerned with portraying an interior reality, in the French neo-classical tradition, and exterior reality is secondary to this intention.

Crébillon's treatment of time brings out this aspect. In his introduction to his own story, Meilcour explains his relations, or lack of them, with Madame de Lursay: 'Nous soupirions tous deux en secret; et, quoique d'accord, nous n'en étions pas plus heureux' (p.76). This unsatisfactory situation had continued for at least two months previously before Madame de Lursay decided to resolve the matter to mutual advantage. This will take fourteen days to accomplish (Etiemble says fifteen days, perhaps meaning a fortnight as an approximate calculation), described in a further one hundred and seventy-two pages.

There is good reason why, although they are in agreement, it will take those further fourteen days for them to reach the sexual *dénouement*, for the social game of coquetry and desire in this text is perpetually out of synchronisation, as will later be the case to similarly comic effect in any nineteenth-century French farce. The couple formed by Madame de Lursay and Meilcour is that of a woman perfectly aware of the code of behaviour, and anxious to observe it, involved with a young man totally unaware of what is expected of him in society. The memorialist observes analytically the effects of his behaviour at that time: he misunderstands the signals of encouragement sent to him; he fails to take advantage of the opportunities presented to him; later, he tactlessly and brusquely demands those favours previously offered to him without a positive reaction on his part. However, his naivety and the slow pace of the seduction make him even more desirable and he will be forgiven when he reaches the anticipated conclusion.

Time is used to advantage to convey to the reader the sense that the situation could move rapidly to an anticipated conclusion and yet it moves slowly and without the finesse expected in players of the game. The female partner, accustomed to a role of feigned resistance, is obliged to conduct the intrigue entirely on her own and for the most part in vain; the male partner maintains a comic passivity in the course of his slow initiation and shows none of the intellectual qualities that are frequently seen as a distinguishing feature of the libertine genre and described by the striking phrase 'romanesque de l'intelligence'.

It may be added that Crébillon's handling of time is similar to Marivaux's treatment, both concerned with detail and a pattern of closely succeeding events. These events are everyday activities, but since both Marivaux and Crébillon are concerned entirely with personal relationships and their effect on the protagonists, reflection takes up more time within the text than the events themselves. In Crébillon's case, a better balance is achieved because of his emphasis on conversation.

5. The Art of Conversation

It has already been suggested that *Les Egarements* is particularly suitable for transference to the stage. This is because of the large proportion of the text that consists of scenes of dialogue. The reader is expected to believe that the memorialist Meilcour is able to recall with complete accuracy conversations between a number of participants several years previously, more than half the text indeed consisting of dialogue.

Moreover, the conversations relayed express the art of conversation among people accustomed to using language in a particular way developed by their exclusive society. Language, like everything else, is subject to implicit rules. Such language and especially wit, sometimes exploited to excess of artificiality, are important elements in that sociability which is an important feature of the period.

Philip Stewart, in an important study of the language of love in the French eighteenth century, begins from the premise that 'la dimension analytique de la langue parlée dans la haute société du XVIIIe siècle est compromise par l'élaboration d'un art de la conversation caractérisé par un degré élevé de raffinement, mais aussi de convention' (*35*, p.9).

There is an intimate connection between elegant conversation and that *amour-goût* defined and analysed by Crébillon. Language is much concerned with the game of love, which does not distinguish between love and pleasure. The mask of language conceals the true meaning that will be transposed into the sexual act. Stewart sees *les gradations* of the game of love not as a technique of seduction but rather as the steps of a ritual dance, which, of course, Meilcour needs to learn. The dancers will then reach the 'moment', the point of mutual gratification. Since it is a skill that requires to be perfected, Stewart describes Meilcour as learning a language in a novel which 'tourne tout entier autour de l'art de converser, et presque toutes les situations de l'intrigue sont en effet des conversations. Le héros

Meilcour ... n'a rien de plus important à faire que de parler et d'apprendre à mieux parler' (*35*, p.160). He will need the help of both Madame de Lursay and Versac to understand the principles underlying the social art of conversation. Madame de Lursay will bring him to the act of sexual initiation by means of a scene of verbal mastery, of language used as a weapon to dominate the initiate. Versac also dominates, in his case an entire social group, by disguising his intellectual ability and using language to impose his own supremacy. He masks his own ideas and aims by using conventional language with total cynicism.

There exists the necessity for a particular form of language. Crébillon's characters, especially the women, use language to avoid control by an ever-watchful society that condemns pleasures they enjoy and is always ready to destroy reputations. Meilcour, as narrator, comments in his introduction on the disguised meaning of the language of love that must be used in society: 'Avec un homme expérimenté, un mot dont le sens même peut se détourner, un regard, un geste, moins encore, le met au fait, s'il veut être aimé; et, supposé qu'il se soit arrangé différemment de ce qu'on souhaiterait, on n'a hasardé que des choses si équivoques, et de si peu de conséquence, qu'elles se désavouent sur-le-champ' (p.76). Versac will teach him that worldly success is based on use of language. Even when society people express definite ideas on the sentiment of love, the analysis of love is only a game played in the *salons* since the early seventeenth century and does not necessarily indicate sincerity of feeling. The language of preciosity inherited from the seventeenth century becomes a sentimental and worldly jargon whose underlying meaning is often different from the term used, as *amour* frequently corresponds with the more fleeting *désir*.

This usage provides Crébillon with the opportunity to satirise representative characters such as Madame de Senanges through the ironic remarks of his libertine Versac. 'Non, répondit-elle, pour prude, je ne crois pas que je la devienne, cela n'est pas de mon caractère; mais je vous avouerai que je hais l'indécence. Etre indécente, est une chose qui me révolte, et que je ne pardonne pas. On ne saurait penser autrement quand on est aussi bien née que vous l'êtes, répondit-il d'un air sérieux' (p.194). The hypocrisy of the libertine Madame de Senanges is emphasised by Versac's irony.

At the same time, irony is not limited to the libertine characters and Madame de Lursay brings out Meilcour's deficiencies through her mockery: 'C'est le plaisir de vous confondre, de dévoiler votre mauvaise foi, vos caprices, et de vous faire enfin rougir de vous-même' (p.237). Her stated conclusion, which elucidates society's code of conduct, is unambiguous: 'Vous ignorez avec les femmes, jusqu'à la façon dont on doit leur parler' (p.235).

In earlier scenes, Madame de Lursay makes every effort to obtain from Meilcour an open avowal of his feelings for her, while maintaining the ambiguity of her feminine discourse. For his part, he remains incapable of seeing the efforts she makes to encourage him: 'ne connaissant pas la différence qu'il y a entre une femme vertueuse, et une prude, il n'était point étonnant que je n'attendisse pas de Madame de Lursay plus de facilité qu'elle ne se disait capable d'en avoir' (p.95).

Hortense, on the rare occasions when she converses with Meilcour, expresses herself in a very different style. The young girl is concerned to know more about love, just like one of Marivaux's heroines, but has only read about it in books. On her entry into society, she speaks the language of true love, the *tendresse* she anticipates, and revealingly expresses her fears ('Pensez-vous donc, … qu'une passion mutuelle ne soit pas le comble du malheur, lorsque tout s'oppose à sa félicité?', p.173). Such obstacles are placed by society in the path of those who seek real affection and indeed Hortense and Meilcour will not overcome them.

Versac continually returns to the subject of love-affairs, his own and those of others, and inevitably he refers to *amour-goût*. In the course of conversation, Madame de Mongennes enquires whether he still has 'quelque tendre engagement' with 'la petite de ***'. He responds nonchalantly that 'il serait un peu difficile ... que ce fût toujours elle. Je ne l'ai jamais eue. Ah! quelle folie, s'écria Madame de Mongennes, dénier une affaire aussi publique, et dont tout le monde se tue de parler depuis deux mois!' (p.193). While Versac denies one liaison, he admits to others without ambiguity: 'j'en ai fini une ce matin' and another begins immediately: 'j'imaginais pourtant que le fait était déjà public. Cela s'est commencé très vivement à l'Opéra, continué ailleurs, et cela s'achève aujourd'hui dans ma petite maison' (ibid.).

The conversation is maintained by discussion of Versac's invitation to those present to attend a reception in his *petite maison*, a residence usually reserved for private assignations. Madame de Mongennes expresses her delight at the invitation in society jargon, 'cela est galant au possible', but Madame de Senanges objects that such a venue would be indecent and worthy of censure by society. This intervention will allow Versac not only to proclaim the charms of the *petite maison* as well as the necessary role it plays in society but also to satirise Madame de Senanges and her feigned obeisance to virtuous and acceptable behaviour.

Versac addresses Madame de Lursay 'du ton le plus insolent et de l'air le plus familier' (p.136), but nevertheless she considers it prudent to persuade him to remain in her *salon* when he announces his departure, using worldly jargon in her insincere protestations that mask her detestation of him: 'Ah, comte! s'écria Madame de Lursay, quelle cruauté! Quoi vous partez! Il y a mille ans que je ne vous ai vu; vous resterez' (p.138).

Indeed, as Meilcour remarks when he begins to describe the scene as he sits down to supper at the residence of Madame de Lursay, 'ce ton charmant qu'on appelle le ton de la bonne compagnie, n'est le plus souvent que le ton de l'ignorance, du précieux et de l'affectation. Ce fut le ton de notre souper' (p.154). It is the scene of dialogue (pp.153-64) that Philippe Berthier describes as 'Le Souper impossible' (*16*). This title indicates the author's view that the scene described is one of impossibility of communication between the participants:

> Théoriquement lieu de partage, ... il s'éprouve ici comme une rencontre de la vacuité. La finalité de la table est complètement pervertie puisque, au lieu d'inviter à la consommation d'un même aliment, ... elle convie à éprouver l'absence. On ne se nourrit que de langage, et d'un langage qui affirme vigoureusement, agressivement (sous les manières souriantes de la 'bonne compagnie')

> les tensions et les divorces. Au menu du souper, il n'y a
> que la parole, et une parole qui sépare. (*16*, p.76)

Three men and four women sit down to supper, placing
themselves as they wish. However, they are limited in their choice
and they do so each with the intention of attack or defence: Pranzi
directs his intended witticisms at Madame de Lursay, Madame de
Senanges seeks to capture Meilcour, Versac has been prevented from
seating himself next to Hortense by the combined strategy of
Madame de Lursay and Madame de Théville.

Apart from the contrived element of their placing, the
characters' conversation reflects their intentions towards each other.
Versac discusses various topics specifically with Madame de
Senanges and Madame de Lursay, but these are without any special
interest to any of the three of them, the subject-matter simply
reflecting the tone of polite conversation, which habitually revolves
around love in all its aspects. Versac would prefer to be speaking
with Hortense, who is lost in deep reverie. The two ladies, while
conversing with Versac, each hopes to influence Meilcour in her
favour. Meilcour and Hortense are joined in mutual silence. It is
indeed symbolic that the dialogue is insincere, but that the
expression of the sincerity of feelings of the two young people is
indicated through their silence. If Hortense truly despises Meilcour
for his apparent sudden interest in Madame de Senanges, which she
is not to know is done to spite Madame de Lursay, the young girl's
seeming contempt is seen only through the expression in her eyes.

An abstract and generalised form of conversation is habitually
used in the salons, 'c'est qu'il y a, reprit Madame de Senanges, des
femmes qui ne savent ce que c'est que se respecter' (p.155) and 'il
est des femmes dont je pense on ne peut pas plus mal' (p.157), as
Versac states, and there is often a *sous-entendu* applicable to those
present in these apparent generalisations. Versac particularly is a past
master at stating the truth of immorality that lies beneath the mask of
language. On this occasion, he is joined paradoxically by Madame de
Théville, portrayed as a woman of severe virtue, who is disinclined
by temperament to be anything but frank.

Versac, here as elsewhere in the text, takes on the role of
spokesman for Crébillon's criticisms of society. He states and

develops an unmentionable truth, 'les femmes se rendent promptement, à peine attendent-elles qu'on les en prie' (p.157) and with total cynicism he takes advantage of this behaviour because he is amoral. The frankness of his statements proves shocking to his hearers, especially those who have something in their conduct to conceal, and it offends against the social code of language as deception.

This scene is the most striking example of dialogue between a number of participants, including all the important characters in the text, bringing to light individual motivations that lie beneath the surface of the dialogue. At the same time, it affords Crébillon the opportunity of a bitter satire against society.

Two other scenes within this text are analysed by Carole Dornier in her discussion of the rhetoric of *libertinage* (20). The first examines the manipulation of Meilcour by Madame de Lursay to persuade him to declare his feelings for her (pp.76-84). The narrator sets out the problem facing Madame de Lursay in his introduction to the scene: 'Il s'agissait de me mettre au-dessus de la défiance qu'elle m'avait donnée de moi-même, et de la trop bonne opinion qu'elle m'avait fait prendre d'elle; ... Elle ne voyait point d'apparence que j'osasse lui déclarer que je l'aimais; et loin qu'elle dût prendre sur elle de se découvrir, elle était forcée de paraître recevoir avec sévérité l'aveu que je lui ferais, si encore elle était assez heureuse pour m'amener jusque-là ' (p.76). Madame de Lursay manipulates the conversation that follows with the intention of obtaining from Meilcour a declaration of his feelings for her, but equally only too well aware of his timidity. She therefore makes it easy for him, but conceals her motives.

The initial subject of conversation between them is a recent play containing a scene of declaration of love, and a shared appreciation of the dramatist's handling of this theme allows Madame de Lursay to make the generalised statement that it is a situation that occurs frequently and is perfectly easy to carry out. This permits Meilcour to move the conversation, still in general terms, to his perceived belief that, on the contrary, it is difficult to make such a declaration. Madame de Lursay distinguishes between the ease with which men are able to make an overture and its

unconventionality, that is to say its unacceptability, when coming
from a woman, which constitutes an encouragement to Meilcour in
his specific case, even though it remains a generalised remark based
on the experience of an older person, aware of the requirements of
bienséance. This also makes clear to Meilcour that it is impossible
for her to declare her feelings to him and that he must take the
initiative, regardless of his fear of the possibly embarrassing
consequences.

Even when the young man cites himself as an example,
Madame de Lursay's response remains impersonal: 'Eh! comptez-
vous pour rien, Madame, repris-je, l'embarras de le dire, surtout pour
moi qui sens que je le dirais mal? Les déclarations les plus élégantes
ne sont pas toujours, répondit-elle, les mieux reçues. On s'amuse de
l'esprit d'un amant, mais ce n'est pas lui qui persuade' (p.79).

Madame de Lursay makes every effort to persuade, this being
indeed the rhetoric of *libertinage*, and to bring Meilcour to tell her
what she wishes to hear: 'Il est plus avantageux, même plus
raisonnable, de parler, que de s'obstiner à se taire. Vous risquez de
perdre, par le silence le plaisir de vous savoir aimé; et si l'on ne peut
vous répondre comme vous le voudriez, vous vous guérissez d'une
passion inutile qui ne fera jamais que votre malheur' (ibid.).

Above all, Madame de Lursay must be seen by her companion
merely as an advisor and not as someone competent to commit
herself as to the outcome of the desired declaration of love.
Nevertheless, when the moment is right, she will abandon
generalised instruction in favour of an 'obligeante réflexion', as the
narrator puts it: 'Je remarque que depuis longtemps vous me parlez
sur ce sujet: et, si je ne me trompe, une déclaration ne vous paraît
embarrassante, que parce que vous en avez une à faire' (ibid.) The
tone of disinterest is maintained, remaining the attitude merely of
friendly counsel: 'Je veux d'abord que vous me disiez quel est votre
choix; jeune et sans expérience, comme vous êtes, peut-être l'avez-
vous fait trop légèrement' (p.80). Meilcour is therefore forced to
respond and the conditional form of that response does not make it
any the less clear as to who is the object of his declaration. 'Ah!
Madame, répondis-je en tremblant, je serais bientôt puni de vous
l'avoir dit' (ibid.). The supposition becomes even clearer with the
admission that it may be 'une personne telle que vous que j'aimasse'

and finally the concealment is abandoned: 'Oserais-je donc, Madame, vous dire que je ne suppose rien?' (p.81).

Madame de Lursay has succeeded, through the use of generalisation and hypothesis in this controlled dialogue, in bringing Meilcour to the point of making the declaration required to begin a liaison in due form and he is so bemused by what he has been led to say that he actually believes he has annoyed Madame de Lursay and wishes he had not spoken: 'J'avais si peu d'usage du monde, que je crus l'avoir fâchée véritablement. Je ne savais pas qu'une femme suit rarement une conversation amoureuse avec quelqu'un qu'elle veut engager' (p.83).

The second scene analysed by Carole Dornier within this text is certainly one of the most important. It is the scene in which Meilcour is given a lesson in worldly behaviour by Versac (pp.206-23). The knowledge given is founded on general principles expressed in the form of precepts, with the intention of providing Meilcour with the rules needed for worldly success, as a substitute for any views he might have held of a moral nature. At the centre of this worldly lesson is the concept that it is less dangerous to lack feelings than manners. Dagen (p.260, n.117) reminds the reader that such distinctions are similar to those made by the moralist La Bruyère, while it is also possible to find close similarities in La Rochefoucauld's *Maximes* (1665). It is stated explicitly and also implicitly within the lesson that *bienséance* takes precedence over morality. All this is expressed in a generalised form that adopts the maxim, but also the imperative, to reinforce Versac's advice. It is in any case the tone of the libertine who dominates his society, even to the extent of voluntary deformation of his personality to achieve a contrived perfection in the manner of the stage actor.

Versac seeks indeed to manipulate Meilcour's whole view of life. It is essential to his worldly success that Meilcour will have a view of women that seeks their seduction through careful study of their weaknesses, the appearance of feeling for them allied with a total absence of genuine sentiment, fulfilling the actor's role before a female audience.

This scene takes the form of a lecture, or rather a tutorial, more than a dialogue. After a discussion during which Versac attempts to

persuade Meilcour of the social necessity for him to undertake a
liaison with Madame de Senanges, a subject to which Versac returns
at the end of their meeting, leaving Meilcour unconvinced, for the
remainder of the scene their talk is entirely one-sided. 'Permettez-
moi une question, lui dis-je, ne soyez même pas surpris si dans le
cours de cette conversation, je vous en fais quelques-unes. Vous me
dites des choses qui me sont trop nouvelles, pour que je les saisisse
d'abord comme vous le voudriez' (p.208). In this way, by question
and answer, Meilcour obtains an explanation of the meaning of 'les
ridicules en crédit' (p.210) as part of 'l'art de plaire' in relation to
women. When Versac explains to him the elements of the skill of the
great actor on the worldly stage, 'Etre passionné sans sentiment,
pleurer sans être attendri, tourmenter sans être jaloux; voilà tous les
rôles que vous devez jouer', Meilcour doubts whether his own
abilities are equal to the task: 'Ce détail est étonnant, lui dis-je, il
m'effraie, je sens que je ne pourrai jamais en porter le poids' (p.216).

After a lengthy commentary of explanation as to what is meant
by 'le ton de la vraiment bonne compagnie' (p.221), Versac prepares
to undertake a dissertation on women as part of his 'Traité de
Morale' (p.222), but he decides to put this off to another occasion,
which never occurs within the text. They return instead to the vexed
question of why Meilcour needs Madame de Senanges to initiate him
into society, then they part, Meilcour informing us that he returned
home 'sans faire beaucoup de réflexions à tout ce que Versac
m'avait dit' (p.223).

Nevertheless, even though Meilcour the protagonist apparently
minimises the importance of the scene, perhaps because he is still
incensed at Versac's insistence on Madame de Senanges, the reader
must conclude that it has had a decisive formative influence. The
young man is not sufficiently experienced to put this lesson into
practice when faced with Madame de Lursay in the final scene of the
novel. However, the scene does serve to explain the thought-
processes of the libertine through his own utterance, for Crébillon
chooses the spoken word to set out a psychological and moral lesson.
The words of the libertine show the reader what Meilcour will
become, while implicitly and effectively criticising the libertine
system. Versac unmasked, since he feels free to speak openly before
an audience too young to pose an immediate threat, is able to explain

lucidly his inner contempt for society and his desire to dominate and manipulate that same society through the very falseness of its code of behaviour. Here lies the importance of the brief exchange at the beginning of the lesson: 'Quoi! lui dis-je en riant, vous pourriez être fâché que je disse *Versac sait penser*? Sans doute, répliqua-t-il fort sérieusement, et vous saurez bientôt pourquoi il m'est important que vous ne le disiez pas' (p.209).

The setting for the dialogue that forms so great a part of this text is undoubtedly the *salons*. Whether the scene of dialogue recounted by Crébillon's narrator takes place in a society drawing-room, or in a dining-room, or on a walk in the Tuileries gardens or the Etoile, or, as in the culminating scene, in a lady's boudoir, the tone and subject-matter of conversation are those of the *salon*.

As has already been indicated, Crébillon's formative influences were the *coulisses* of the theatre and his entrée to theatrical performances through his father's reputation and contacts in theatrical circles, but also particularly his attendance as an *habitué* of *salon* society through his father's social contacts. An analysis of his literary work suggests also that he possessed an innate capacity for observation of speakers and their dialogue. Contemporary critics of Crébillon were unanimous, whatever their critical attitudes to his works, in declaring that he accurately captured the conversation of the society that he sought to portray. This is particularly relevant in the case of *Les Egarements du cœur et de l'esprit*, where a realistic and true reflection of the 'vraiment bonne compagnie' is clearly the intention of the author, who could not otherwise have achieved his satiric effects.

The very fact that so great a proportion of the text is dialogue means that characters are established by means of their speech. While they are normally introduced by a brief verbal portrait provided by the narrator, a transference to the novel of a pastime of the *salon*, the characters then develop their role within the plot in terms of what they have to say. Their language takes various forms, as has been suggested: beneath the lucidity of witty expression and analysis often lies a strategy of attack or defence, a need to disguise one's real intentions, a vocabulary that is coded for interpretation by a circle of initiates, and language which is above all the weapon, when deployed by Crébillon's characters, to achieve a seduction.

The use of speech in this text differentiates it superficially from other works by Crébillon written in epistolary form, such as the *Lettres de la Marquise de M*** au Comte de R**** (1732), or the *Lettres de la Duchesse de *** au Duc de **** (1768), or the *Lettres athéniennes* (1771), a form that remained popular throughout the eighteenth century and to which Crébillon returned from 1732 to the end of his writing career in 1771. In these epistolary novels, the characters establish themselves necessarily through their letters, from the Marquise's univocal correspondence to the fictional letters by a selection of correspondents written in the setting of a pseudo-classical Greece. What needs to be stressed is that the style used by Crébillon for all of these correspondents is that of *langue parlée*.

It should also be remembered that, among the most successful of Crébillon's published works, to which he returned continuously over a number of years before presenting them for publication, were the 'dialogues' *La Nuit et le moment ou les Matines de Cythère, dialogue* (1755) and *Le Hasard du coin du feu, dialogue moral* (1763), both of which take the form of a conversation between two protagonists and conclude with an inevitable seduction, their words achieving the aim, unstated but mutually understood, of the reality of sexual gratification, achieved in the most socially acceptable manner.

6. Reception

Within the French novel of the eighteenth century, Crébillon has a unique place. However, his reputation has varied considerably within his own lifetime and since his death. Conroy comments that 'after wide acclaim and redounding success in the eyes of his contemporaries for his earlier works, he seems to have outlived his talent, producing works after 1750 which no longer found a receptive audience' (*18*, p.9). This despite Conroy's view that 'of all the novelists in the first half of the eighteenth century, Crébillon manifests the most interest in novelistic processes and techniques, the sharpest feeling for the novel as a literary form' (*18*, p.12). It could have been expected that interest in Crébillon's literary works and ideas on the novel would have been maintained after 1750, for Diderot was influenced by Crébillon in his writing of *Les Bijoux indiscrets*, Sterne was much impressed by his work and the form and characterisation of Laclos's *Les Liaisons dangereuses* owe a great deal to Crébillon.

Siemek mentions contemporaries of Crébillon who praised his works, among them Voltaire, d'Alembert and Palissot, and 'on trouve aussi de nombreux jugements favorables de la presse littéraire, surtout pour les œuvres publiées dans les années trente. Les opinions négatives portent, bien entendu, sur la frivolité et l'érotisme, mais le plus souvent elles concernent les dernières œuvres (1754-1771) jugées ennuyeuses et maniérées. De l'avis commun, Crébillon est un auteur qui survit à sa gloire' (*33*, p.17).

It is interesting therefore that these two important modern critics are agreed on Crébillon's literary value, but also on his decline after 1750. From the outset, there were contemporary critics who blamed Crébillon for the eroticism in his work, among whom were La Mettrie, Madame du Deffand and La Harpe. Others, such as l'Abbé Desfontaines, see the *libertinage crébillonien* as indicative merely of the accepted frivolity, the wit and the rococo style of his period. Palissot praises Crébillon as a moralist for portraying and satirising the vices of his time and illustrating the libertine code of behaviour. The ambiguities of style dear to Crébillon and deemed necessary by him to achieve the depiction of a certain society were condemned by Palissot, and Diderot introduces into his *Bijoux indiscrets* the character of Girgiro l'Entortillé to parody that style.

I have suggested elsewhere *(25)* in an essay specifically concerned with the study of the feminine characters in certain eighteenth-century novels, the division of the novels for consideration into novels of sensibility and novels of *libertinage*; nevertheless, it was pointed out that any absolute distinction of that nature, of which the authors were not cognizant, is artificial. In Crébillon's case, however, there is no doubt that his works must be placed within the genre of the novel of *libertinage*, but certain critics' preferences for the novel of sensibility may well account for their negative reaction to the content and style of his works and equally for the lack of popularity from which he suffered in the second half of the eighteenth century owing to changes in literary taste.

Sensibility and Romanticism as attitudes and codes of behaviour existed even before their literary manifestations and this no doubt explains in part the immediate success of works such as Rousseau's *La Nouvelle Héloïse* in 1761. But long before this date, there is a development in the novel from the seventeenth to the eighteenth centuries that leads from preciosity to sensibility, with elements of preciosity remaining in the *roman de sensibilité*. Equally, there are distinctions between the novels of Prévost, Marivaux, Diderot, Rousseau and Bernardin de Saint-Pierre within the genre of the novel of sensibility.

Crébillon's works form part of the genre of the psychological novel and they also illustrate cerebral *libertinage*, for which he may be considered as the author of the libertine code expressed through characters such as Versac. The libertine characters of Laclos, Merteuil and Valmont, follow that code and expressly bring out the aspect of cruelty in their behaviour towards their victims, which is already latent in Crébillon's view of his world.

It may be true that the genre of the novel of *libertinage* had been displaced by 1750 in literary fashion and public taste by the novel of sensibility until the decline of that genre after it found its final major expression with the publication in 1788 of *Paul et Virginie* by Bernardin de Saint-Pierre. Laclos's *Les Liaisons dangereuses*, the masterpiece of the novel of cerebral *libertinage*, was a *succès de scandale*, to be succeeded by the works of Sade, taking *libertinage* in a different direction. At the same time, the novel of sensibility, with which Sade had certain undeniable affinities, developed into the Romantic novel, again following a different code and series of attitudes.

As regards Crébillon's literary fortunes, it has to be remembered that the aristocratic setting of his novels and the attitudes expressed by his characters remain to the end firmly rooted in the period of the Regency of 1715-23. This is perfectly realistic for the readership of *Les Egarements du cœur et de l'esprit* of 1736-38, where the memorialist is describing his entry into Regency society and the behaviour of the society of which he was to form part.

However, it is this same society and its attitudes towards pleasure that provides the true setting for much later work published in the 1750s, 1760s and even until 1771. This may account for the accusations of frivolity levelled against Crébillon for the tone of his later works, even though it differs little from those written earlier in the century. We read Crébillon today as a social commentator illustrating the Regency period; moreover, we see the code of behaviour he formulated and the behaviour he described as leading gradually to the changes in public opinion that culminated in the Revolution of 1789. It is in this sense that modern critics view Crébillon's importance as a moralist.

The libertine that Crébillon portrays is a product of the Regency and the code by which he lives influences his successors throughout the century, including Valmont in *Les Liaisons dangereuses*. It must be recognised, however, that the character of the libertine is of all time, that the myth of Don Juan, with its roots in the Spanish literary tradition, is not an invention of the eighteenth century, although it is particularly appropriate to the *chasse au plaisir* of that period, with its infinite repetition of the game of seduction. Richardson's character Lovelace is an obvious example of Don Juan's English posterity. The tradition of *libertinage* inevitably continues into the nineteenth century, even though the models of the libertine and the dandy differ. Byron's Don Juan found an echo in Musset's *Lorenzaccio*, although Musset drew on his own experience even more than Byron.

Within the libertine genre, *Les Egarements du cœur et de l'esprit* has a major place, as much a masterpiece of the memoir-form as *Les Liaisons dangereuses* is the successful culmination of the epistolary novel. This memoir-form, made popular at the beginning of the century by Hamilton among others with his *Mémoires de la vie du comte de Grammont*, is used to supreme effect by Crébillon, with the memorialist and his younger self combining to illuminate for the reader the personality of Meilcour as a youth and what he has become within his society.

As with any novel of the libertine genre, the psychological insight of the narrator is focused on a single central theme, that of seduction. In the preface, Crébillon states 'l'amour seul préside ici' (p.68) and Meilcour analyses the nature of the only kind of love that can realistically exist within his society, while personally regretting explicitly at the end of the text the impossibility of a successful outcome for the relationship he would have preferred to have with Hortense.

Besides the technical advantages he gains from the memoir-form, Crébillon uses the narrator Meilcour to provide a view, through representative types, of the restricted society that he wishes to depict. This is achieved through the introductory portraits of such characters and then through the recall of dialogue by the narrator as they reveal themselves through their speech. This text is exceptional in the extent to which direct speech is used, giving it a theatrical quality. The reader sees in action the libertines, men and women, the prude, the young girl, the virtuous and the dissolute, moral and amoral, all brought together in the *salon*, where the action is essentially psychological.

In the evolution of *libertinage*, Crébillon marked the first step, as the author of a libertine code, which later writers were to take further, but never to efface. He was among the first novelists to exploit the theme of *sensibilité* versus *libertinage*; he implies the moral superiority of the former, although the latter may prevail in practice. What interests him is to explore the impact of *libertinage*, which he equates with corruption and decadence, on individual human beings. The thesis of H.-G. Funke, which unfortunately remains untranslated from the German, is devoted to Crébillon as a moralist and critic of society and strongly expresses the opinion that Crébillon intended to express a negative view of this society, to condemn *amour-goût* and its casuistry and to advocate virtuous and sincere love, as Siemek has noted (*33*, pp.21-22).

Clearly, Meilcour exalts his feelings for Hortense over his relations with Madame de Lursay; from his first meeting with Hortense, his passion is described as if he were the hero of a *roman de sensibilité*. His emotions control him to the point that he sometimes appears comic, if not ridiculous, in his behaviour, not only towards Hortense but also when he believes he has strong feelings for Madame de Lursay. Indeed, when initially Meilcour is describing Madame de Lursay, together with her way of thought, he brings out the fact that 'son système n'était point, qu'on ne dût pas avoir des faiblesses, mais que le sentiment seul pouvait les rendre pardonnables' (p.74). This presumably indicates that, whatever the narrator knows about her conduct, she places sentiment above *libertinage*; she tries to inspire genuine feelings for her in Meilcour and when she finally gives herself to him, the *cri de cœur* from this mature woman for whom this will be the last liaison is the pathetic 'je suis perdue, si je ne suis pas heureuse' (p.245). The way that Crébillon depicts his libertine characters, Madame de Senanges, Versac and Pranzi, accentuates their decadence and, in the case of Versac, his dissatisfaction in the midst of his social success, that he should be obliged to conceal his intelligence and personal qualities.

Crébillon wrote *Les Egarements du cœur et de l'esprit* at the same period as Duclos's *Les Confessions du Comte de* ***. An obvious distinction between them is that the tone of Duclos's novel changes completely and, from a typical example of the libertine genre, becomes a novel of sensibility. In his preface, Crébillon announces a future for Meilcour similar to that of the Comte 'rendu à lui-même, devoir toutes ses vertus à une femme estimable' (p.68). It may be concluded that Crébillon realised he had already found a more realistic conclusion.

It is a fact that the libertine code accepted and executed in practice by Laclos's characters Merteuil and Valmont was already long-established within the genre in recognition of Crébillon. Laclos's masterly innovation was the invention of Madame de Merteuil, a female libertine more dangerous than the male. The erotic content of Laclos's work is part of the libertine genre and already found in Crébillon, but in both cases the novelist is concerned with the mental processes of his characters rather than scenes of sexual prowess.

Sade attempts to justify the libertine behaviour of his characters on grounds of Nature and Reason. For him, whatever exists in Nature must necessarily be natural and Reason must lead to domination and victimisation of the weak by the strong in the libertine tradition. There is already to be found in Crébillon a justification for libertine behaviour through Reason based on determinism, scepticism, hedonism and the acknowledged weakness of the flesh.

In Sade's works, the logic of these theoretical positions is taken to their furthest extent through the discourse of his libertines, who then apply their philosophy of victimisation in scenes of physical torture. However, there is a reaction against *libertinage* and its scenes of horror as the century progresses because the effects of sensibility suggested to many that *libertinage* was neither in Nature nor in Reason. In any case, it became clear, as was confirmed by the excesses of the Revolution of 1789, and the Terror, that there should be sought a balance between *esprit* and *cœur*.

Libertinage in the nineteenth century is to be found in works such as *Adolphe* (1816) by Benjamin Constant, for this author is much influenced by the heritage of the eighteenth century, but his novel is also affected by Romanticism and it portrays a different form of *libertinage*. As the novelist uses the memoir-form, it becomes obvious that the narrator is suffering from Romantic *mal du siècle*, an excessive sensibility, and his harsh treatment of the heroine Ellénore is more due to weakness and lack of will-power than *libertinage froid*.

It has already been stated that the twentieth century has seen a resurgence of interest in Crébillon's works. Lièvre published in 1929-30 an edition of the *Œuvres complètes* that includes the most important works. Etiemble published a scholarly edition of *Les Egarements du cœur et de l'esprit* in the Gallimard Pléiade series in 1965. He saw himself as the champion of Crébillon in rehabilitating his literary reputation, and in the Introduction to his edition of *Les Egarements* published by Colin in 1961, stated that the text should be compulsory reading for all adolescents. While he was clearly thinking of French adolescents, who are allegedly endowed with more analytical minds and whose literary culture contains examples of the theme of initiation of an adolescent by a mature woman, Anglo-Saxon youth might well also benefit from his recommendation.

The education of the young involves awareness of the problems of the interplay of sexual motivation, emotion and reason, and the mixed messages conveyed. There is always a code of conduct and language which needs to be deciphered correctly to avoid error on the part of the unwary. This code, the whole pattern of relationships, changes from generation to generation, but there is always a pattern which, if ignored, necessarily leads to misunderstanding and disaster. The game of love and lust takes on different facets in different periods of history, but the basic moves are the same. In this way, *Les Egarements* goes well beyond a presentation of an exclusively eighteenth-century way of life, if the underlying message is clearly understood; its combination of eroticism, psychological sophistication, comedy and pastiche make it truly a text for our times.

Select Bibliography

WORKS BY CRÉBILLON FILS

I am indebted to Jean Sgard for the following extracts from the *Catalogue des Oeuvres de Claude Crébillon* established by the group working on the critical edition of the *Oeuvres de Crébillon* (Classiques Garnier). This group includes Michel Gilot and Jacques Rustin for *Les Egarements*. I am grateful to Jean Sgard for providing bibliographical data which has only recently been made available.

1. *Le Sylphe, ou Songe de Madame de R*** écrit par elle-même à Madame de S*** (Paris, L.D. Delatour, 1730).
2. *Lettres de la Marquise de M*** au Comte de R*** (Paris, Prault, 1732).
3. *Tanzaï et Néadarné. Histoire japonaise.* 'A Pékin, Chez Lou-Chou-Lu-La, Seul Imprimeur de Sa Majesté Chinoise pour les langues étrangères' (Paris, Prault?, 1734).
4. *Les Egaremens du cœur et de l'esprit. ou Mémoires de Mr de Meilcour* (Paris, Prault fils, 1re partie, 1736; 2de partie, The Hague, Gosse et Néaulme, 1738; 3e partie, The Hague, Gosse et Néaulme, 1738).

(N.B. There is evidence from Mme de Graffigny, who knew Crébillon well, that he also wrote three further parts that remained unpublished and she refers to these parts twice in her correspondence: 'J'ai persécuté Crébillon pour ces *Egarements*. Il n'est, dit-il, que trop égaré; il en a trois autres parties de finies...', *Correspondance de Mme de Graffigny*, edited by J.A. Dainard and D. Smith for the Voltaire Foundation (6 June 1743, Vol.XXI, p.l93); 'Bon, Crébillon ne veut point donner *Meilcourt*. Il en a trois parties de faite et ne veut point se donner la peine qu'il faut pour les mettre en état d'imprimer. C'est un paresseux plus outré que la paresse même', ibid. (17 March 1744, Vol.XXVII, p.75).

5.   *Le Sopha, conte moral.* 'A Gaznah, de l'Imprimerie du Très-Pieux, Très-Clément et Très-Auguste Sultan des Indes. L'An de l'Hégire. M.C.XX. Avec Privilège du susdit' (Paris, Prault, 1742).
6.   Contribution au *Recueil de ces Messieurs* (Amsterdam, Wetstein frères, 1745).
7.   *Ah, quel conte!* (Brussels, frères Vasse, 1754).
8.   *Les Heureux Orphelins* (Brussels, frères Vasse, 1754).
9.   *La Nuit et le moment ou les Matines de Cythère, dialogue* (London, 1755).
10. *Le Hasard du coin du feu, dialogue moral* (The Hague, 1763).
11. *Lettres de la Duchesse de *** au Duc de **** (London, Jean Nourse, 1768).
12. *Lettres athéniennes extraites du portefeuille d'Alcibiade* (London, Pierre Elsmy and Paris, Delalain, 1771).

THE TEXT

Les Egarements du cœur et de l'esprit appeared in the Gallimard Pléiade edition by Etiemble in 1965, revised in 1987, without changes to the text of the novel. There has been a variety of paperback editions published since 1968, including Etiemble's edition in the Gallimard Folio series (1977) and the Garnier-Flammarion (1985) edited by Jean Dagen, which is perfectly adequate for students and the general reader. Page references are here taken from the Dagen edition, as being generally available.

13. *Romanciers du XVIIIe siècle*, édition d'Etiemble (Paris, Gallimard, Bibliothèque de la Pléiade, new ed. 1987), Vol.II, pp.13-188.
14. Crébillon fils, *Les Egarements du cœur et de l'esprit*, ed. J. Dagen (Paris, GF-Flammarion, No.393, 1985).

CRITICAL STUDIES

15.   Brooks, Peter, *The Novel of Worldliness: Crébillon, Marivaux, Laclos, Stendhal* (Princeton, Princeton University Press, 1969).
16. Berthier, Philippe, 'Le Souper impossible' in *31*, pp.75-85, 95 and 87-88.
17. Cazenobe, Colette, *Le Système du libertinage de Crébillon à Laclos* (Oxford, Voltaire Foundation, Studies on Voltaire and the Eighteenth Century, 282, 1991). (This volume contains a recent bibliography on Crébillon).

18.   Conroy, Peter, *Crébillon fils: techniques of the novel* (Oxford, Voltaire Foundation, Studies on Voltaire and the Eighteenth Century, 99, 1972).

19.   Dagen, Jean, *Introduction à la sophistique amoureuse dans 'Les Egarements du cœur et de l'esprit' de Crébillon fils* (Paris, Champion, Collection Unichamp, 1995).

20.   Dornier, Carole, *Le Discours de maîtrise du libertin* (Paris, Klincksieck, 1994).

21.   Duranton, Henri, 'Le Libertin selon Crébillon, ou les égarements du Chevalier inexistant' in *31*, pp.61-74.

22.   Favre, Robert, 'Les Mémoires d'un oublieux' in *31*, pp.61-74.

23.   Fein, Patrick, 'Crébillon fils, mirror of his society' (Oxford, Voltaire Foundation, Studies on Voltaire and the Eighteenth Century, 88, 1972), pp.485-91.

24.   —— , 'Crébillon fils and eroticism' (Oxford, Voltaire Foundation, Studies on Voltaire and the Eighteenth Century, 152, 1976), pp.723-28.

25.   —— , *Women of sensibility or reason: the function of the feminine characters in the novels of Marivaux, Diderot, Crébillon fils, Duclos and Laclos* (Harare, University of Zimbabwe, 1987).

26.   Gilot, Michel, 'Les doux aveux de Crébillon' in *31*, pp.89-98.

27.   Garagnon, Jean, 'Le maître à penser Versac ou les égarements philosophiques' in *31*, pp.129-49.

28.   Michel, Pierre, '*Les Egarements* ou le roman impossible' in *31*, pp.23-42.

29.   Mylne, Vivienne, *The Eighteenth-Century French Novel: techniques of illusion* (Manchester University Press, 1965).

30.   Niklaus, Robert, 'Crébillon fils et Richardson' (Oxford, Voltaire Foundation, Studies on Voltaire and the Eighteenth Century, 89, 1972), pp.1169-85.

31.   Rétat, Pierre (ed.), *Les Paradoxes du romancier: 'Les Egarements' de Crébillon* (Grenoble, Presses Universitaires de Grenoble, 1975).

32.   Rétat, Pierre, 'Ethique et idéologie dans *Les Egarements*' in *31*, pp.150-59.

33.   Siemek, Andrzej, *Recherche morale et esthétique dans le roman de Crébillon fils* (Oxford, Voltaire Foundation, Studies on Voltaire and the Eighteenth Century, 200, 1981).

34.   Stevens, Marguerite, 'L'Idéalisme et le réalisme dans *Les Egarements du cœur et de l'esprit*' (Oxford, Voltaire Foundation, Studies on Voltaire and the Eighteenth Century, 47, 1966), pp.157-76.

35.   Stewart, Philip, *Le Masque et la parole: le langage de l'amour au XVIIIe siècle* (Paris, José Corti, 1973).

36.   Sturm, Ernest, *Crébillon fils et le libertinage au dix-huitième siècle* (Paris, Nizet, 1970).

37.   Viart, Thierry, *La Convention de l'amour-goût chez Claude Crébillon. Genèse et perspectives* (Oxford, Voltaire Foundation, Studies on Voltaire and the Eighteenth Century, 377, 1999).